CW00690185

MERCHANT & MILLS
SEWING BOOK

MERCHANT & MILLS
SEWING BOOK

 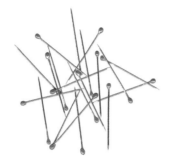 

PROJECTS | TECHNIQUES | GUIDANCE | INSTRUCTIONS
TOOLS | NOTIONS | CHOOSING CLOTH | THE SEWING MACHINE
HAND SEWING | THE ART OF PRESSING | OUR PHILOSOPHY

Carolyn N. K. Denham

WITH WORDS AND PICTURES BY RODERICK FIELD

PAVILION

CONTENTS

PART II: THE TASKS

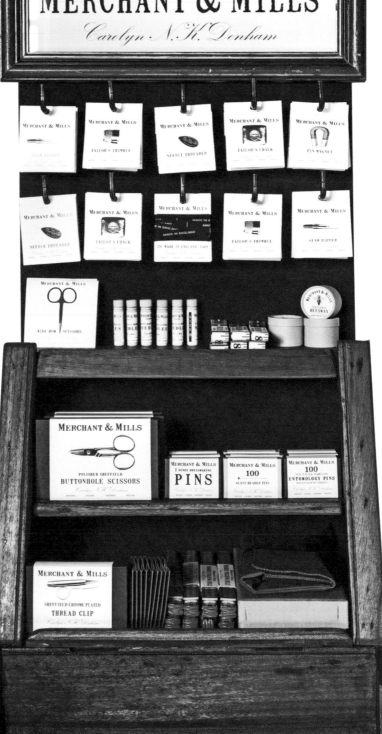

INTRODUCTION

KEEP IT SIMPLE AND DO IT WELL

This book is a condensed volume of the Merchant & Mills take on the art of sewing and the joy of making. It is a response to the questions we are most often asked, and is by no means definitive, yet it clearly reflects our unique way of doing things. Our mission is to enable you to express yourself through textiles, equipped with the necessary skills and knowledge to join the sewing renaissance. These are great times for makers and they will only get better as more of us take up our needles and demand that dressmaking is recognised as a hard earned, respectable skill.

CULINARY LESSONS

Cooking offers some handy parallels for understanding how we approach sewing. Think of the food you might serve at a dinner party. You would neither present your guests with something as humble, plain and simple as porridge, nor present a 15 course Tudor feast on account of the time, planning and expense it would demand. You are more likely to impress your friends with your skills when feeding them your own favourite recipes – the things you love and want to eat, that say something about you. You will make something delicious – and achievable in the time allowed by a busy life.

Whatever you serve, you want it to be desirable and special. Sewing is the same. Make something that you actually want to wear, neither plain as oats nor exotic as stuffed sparrow, but something you can put on with a little glow of pride that says, 'This is me, I made this'. Choose only the best ingredients – from the original pattern to beautiful cloth and the right tools. If this book had to be condensed to just one line, it would say: Keep it simple and do it well.

STITCHES IN TIME

We love sewing and believe in it. The art of sewing provides the invisible thread that literally holds together the world we know. It is everywhere, from the clothes we wear to the sails that enabled the discovery of America. It is in our shoes and bags, the seats on the bus and lurks quietly all around the home. It is best friend to the upholsterer, the seamstress and tailor, the diva and the surgeon, and it is as ancient as time itself. Using animal gut, twine or thread to meld together precedes textiles, reaching back to the very beginnings of humanity when our ancestors sat around the first fire and stitched animal skins together to make up for their own evolutionary lack of fur. Before television, radio and writing, it kept busy the hands of millions, creating warmth, comfort, art and expression. It still does. It employs as many and without it, our world would fray and fall apart.

Yet despite its glorious heritage, the sheer joy and immeasurable satisfaction that making brings seems to have been all but forgotten. The skills that

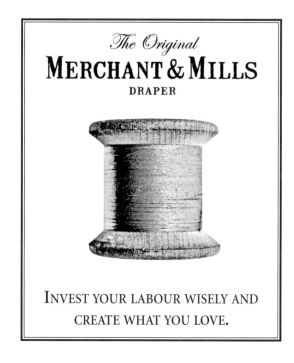

The Original
MERCHANT & MILLS
DRAPER

INVEST YOUR LABOUR WISELY AND CREATE WHAT YOU LOVE.

were once passed down have now been passed by in the name of convenience – something important has been lost. Watch a small child play and it is all about imagination and creation: piling bricks, drawing, cutting and sticking, or discovering the squirmy delights of Plasticine. There is surely nothing more fulfilling than the successful expression of an idea; the alchemy of thoughts becoming things. When we were small, we knew this as fact and we proudly showed the fruits of our efforts, hopefully to much cooing and encouragement. But school takes over and narrows our creativity into narrow channels until we want only to be like everybody else. We forget our unique disposition and quirky style. Later, we have jobs and become a demographic. We are bombarded with standardised goods in every shopping centre and, if we long for the unique, we really have to hunt it out and often pay dearly for it. At Merchant & Mills, we see making not as a poor cousin to shopping but as a way to have long-lasting, beautiful and useful things to be proud of. We want you to spend your time more than your cash and to love the making as much as the result.

To recapture this creative joy and emerge triumphant from the sewing room, there are some skills and techniques that need to be mastered. Do not be afraid. Patience and attentiveness will be rewarded with finished items to be proud of. Keep it simple, do it well, do it once and you will surely earn your outfit. Making is your opportunity to reclaim fashion for yourself.

THE LANGUAGE OF ATTIRE

We cannot speak of sewing without making the leap to fashion. Since history began, the simple technique of stitching has brought us a means of self-expression in which we all participate: the language of attire. Whether we like it or not, what we wear has always made statements about our place in the scheme of things. From shamans to bishops, farmhands to the aristocracy, clothing is used to say something about our identity. It is the most universally seen and interpreted tongue of them all, as it blithely crosses cultures, ignores geographical boundaries and says, 'I am like this'. We cannot step outside this. We all wear clothes and have cushions. Our choices speak.

The essence of mainstream fashion, however, has some difficulties. By its very nature, it is of the moment; the million-dollar creation of yesterday is now hanging abandoned and forlorn in the local Oxfam. Also, in its narrowness, it is determinedly ignoring you, the individual. For a fleeting moment it will insist you have the legs of a baby giraffe or the neck of a swan, and in the High Street you will only find things to fit those unlikely proportions. Fashion, which we hope will say 'look at me, I'm hip', becomes, ironically, a uniform as blatant as a boiler suit or the jeans and T-shirt of those who declare no interest in clothes. And, like all uniforms, it may well not suit you, or it may join you to a club you don't approve of. To add insult to injury, the quality of cloth and construction, at the prices most of us want to pay, is not setting out to win any prizes.

The yen to keep up with what we are told to wear also weighs heavy on the purse and pocket, so drives many of us to make things for ourselves. Yet this also brings up a dilemma for the home dressmaker: is it worth putting in all those hours at the Singer for something that can only be worn for a few months? In search of a resolution, here at Merchant & Mills we take sewing and fashion and we direct these towards something considerably more substantial – classic, timeless style.

From every modern era, there are themes and approaches to assembling garb that withstand the changing weather of fashion and remain steadfast. The clues will lie in the cut, the silhouette, the construction, or simply the designer's unique aesthetic. We all immediately recognise a fashion classic . . . and want it. It is time to make your own.

THE FOUNDATIONS

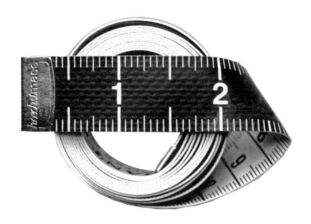

PREPARE TO MAKE WHAT YOU MEAN

SEWING TOOLS

FURNISHING YOUR TOOLBOX

To do any job well, it is of course important to have the right tools to hand. The beginner especially may be tempted to buy every conceivable piece of equipment in the hope that having a freshly painted, dedicated sewing room full of shiny new things will make her an instant seamstress. The sewing tools you actually need are few and unlikely to become obsolete – and the right equipment of 50 years ago is still state of the art today. Good tools are a genuine pleasure to use. In this chapter we look at the items you cannot afford to be without and a few you might want to treat yourself to.

MEASURING AND MARKING

Obvious as it may be, you cannot get very far with sewing tasks without accurate measuring and marking out. If it goes wrong at this early stage you will be struggling through the whole project. For this aspect of making, your attention is just as important as the tools, and nearly anything with calibrated markings can be pressed into service.

THE TAPE MEASURE *(fig. 1, p15)*

Made in anything from paper to woven textile with a PVC coating, there is no shortage of choice with the humble tape measure. They range in cost from a few pence to many pounds. When brand new, any of these will do the job but over time the cheaper ones will stretch significantly. Some tape measures feature a long brass end, which may save some blushes when taking an inside leg measurement, but as this covers the markings on one side of the tape, it can be a bit irritating. Note that tape measures do have a habit of getting lost so make sure you have a back up.

THE GRADER SQUARE *(fig. 2, p15)*

Oh what a joy, especially if you do a lot of pattern alterations. Similar to a school set square, this right-angled triangular wonder is made from transparent plastic; it has centimetres marked along the left-hand edge with corresponding lines marked for the first 5cm parallel to the bottom edge. This makes for simple marking of seam allowances or hems without

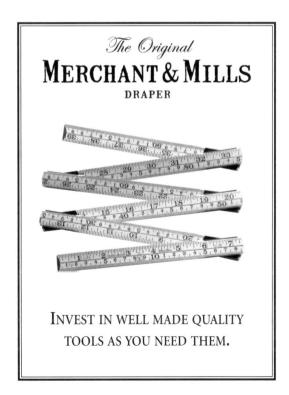

the need to re-measure. It can also be used for instant marking of right angles. Grading rulers are a cheaper option, but they are less versatile and not nearly as clear to use.

SEWING OR HEM GAUGE *(fig. 3)*

This great timesaving device has a moveable pointer allowing for the precise measuring of hems and seam allowances: set it to the desired length, measure and mark, and you're done.

TAILOR'S CHALK *(fig. 4)*

Tailor's chalk resembles an extra slim bar of soap, with nice sharp edges and corners for marking cloth. It comes in various colours to contrast with your fabric and brushes off nicely when the project is completed. Always keep a pencil (Fig 7) handy for pattern marking and notes.

YARDSTICK *(fig. 5)*

This traditional ruler, usually made in wood and now extended to the modern metre, is invaluable for home furnishing projects where long straight lines are needed. As an added bonus it will make you feel like a real tailor when measuring off cloth from the roll. A shorter metal rule can be more manoeuvrable (Fig 6).

SCISSORS

Scissors are the most wondrous invention ever, equalled only perhaps by the bicycle. There are so many scissors on the market, often looking similar but with very different qualities, hence there is a lot of confusion. We have, over the years, tried many of them and narrowed our list down to what works well and will last. Our philosophy when buying scissors is choose wisely and buy once. With scissors 'Buy British' really has some meaning, and the traditional steel city of Sheffield still turns out some of the finest tailor's shears and thread clips that money can buy.

PINKING SHEARS *(fig. 1, p17)*

Specialist scissors with triangular teeth. Contrary to popular belief, these are not multipurpose for all fabrics: they are best suited to tightly woven cloths that are not prone to fraying and they will chew up and destroy loose weave fabrics. A good pair of pinking shears is a rare beast these days, even though all our mothers would have had a pair in the sewing box. They are not cheap and might be considered a real luxury, but cheap alternatives simply do not do the job effectively and are unlikely to last. Quality pinking shears will have a centre bolt so that they can be realigned, as pinkers generally start chewing up fabric when they are misaligned rather than when they are blunt.

WIDE BOW SCISSORS *(fig. 2, p17)*

For snipping threads, trimming and clipping seams. As you will be using these constantly while sewing, choose a good sharp pair with comfortable handles; we like a wide bow handle as it is comfortable to use and offers good leverage. They should be well made and feel precise, with fine blades so that you can snip thread really close to the fabric.

THREAD CLIPS *(fig. 3, p17)*

Designed for snipping threads, these have a finger loop on the bottom and sprung blades. They are an acquired taste: some people swear by them, others find them awkward. If you get on with them they can be incredibly useful as they hang on the third finger, poised and ready for use, gunslinger fashion.

fig. 5 Yardstick

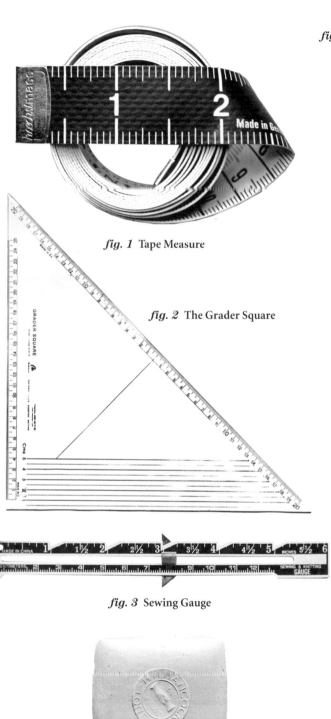

fig. 1 Tape Measure

fig. 6 Metal Ruler

fig. 2 The Grader Square

fig. 7 Pencil

fig. 3 Sewing Gauge

fig. 4 Tailor's Chalk

BUTTONHOLE SCISSORS
(figs. 4a and 4b)

Specialty scissors useful when buttonhole making. There are two types available. The traditional type has a rectangular notch in one blade that allows you to put the scissor over the button placket without cutting it, and they have a screw on the side to regulate the size of the buttonhole. The other type has large handles and short sharp blades, designed to cut through layers of fabric with ease and accuracy. As well as buttonholes these are great for trimming corners and seams where an embroidery scissor isn't strong enough.

TAILOR'S SHEARS *(fig. 5)*

Also known as dressmaking scissors, these are large scissors designed for the accurate cutting out of cloth. Choose the best pair you can afford and the largest pair you can hold comfortably – most commonly these will be 8in (20cm) or, for the brave and confident, 10in (25cm). They can be found for both right-handed and left-handed use. Traditionally, tailor's shears are side bent, which means that the bottom blade of the scissors remains on the table while the upper blade moves to cut. The advantage of this is twofold: firstly the fabric lifts less, making both straight lines and curves eminently more controllable; secondly the support offered by the underlying flat surface means even a heavy shear is not difficult to handle. We prefer a chrome-plated blade, which is smoother than a nickel finish. A good pair of shears can, if needed, be sharpened again and again and will last a lifetime.

Serrated blade tailor's shears are extra sharp. Usually one blade is serrated and the other is a traditional knife-edge. They cut beautifully but can never be sharpened. They tend to be more expensive than traditional dressmaking scissors, making them a more risky investment than standard shears.

PAPER SCISSORS

A separate pair of decent scissors for cutting out paper patterns is essential. Choose a pair with a long and relatively fine blade so that you can cut closely and easily see the cutting line.

SCISSOR CARE

As with any quality item, you will want to take care of your investment. Here are a few top tips:

- ☞ DO NOT use sewing scissors for anything other than cloth as they will quickly blunt and become frustrating to use.
- ☞ Wipe scissor blades with a soft oily cloth after use to remove the build up of tiny dust and fibre particles from between the blades.
- ☞ Avoid dropping your scissors as this can cause irreversible edge damage if the blades are open. Holsters and cases are available for storing scissors safely, or keep them wrapped in soft cloth.
- ☞ You should neither allow the pivot screw to become loose, nor over-tighten it.
- ☞ To prolong the life of your precious scissors and the people you love, keep them out of the reach of children and those who lack respect for nice things.
- ☞ Also, always carry scissors by the blades and don't run with them!

INSIDE INFORMATION

Choose the size of your scissors appropriate to the task at hand. **Big scissors**, or tailor's shears, are for cutting out cloth on a flat surface. **Scissors with short blades** and long shanks (see buttonhole scissors) have extra leverage for cutting through thick material. **Small sharp scissors** are for finer work that requires a high degree of control and accuracy. Using the wrong size scissors causes undue stress, and therefore may not only spoil performance but also shorten the life expectancy of the scissors.

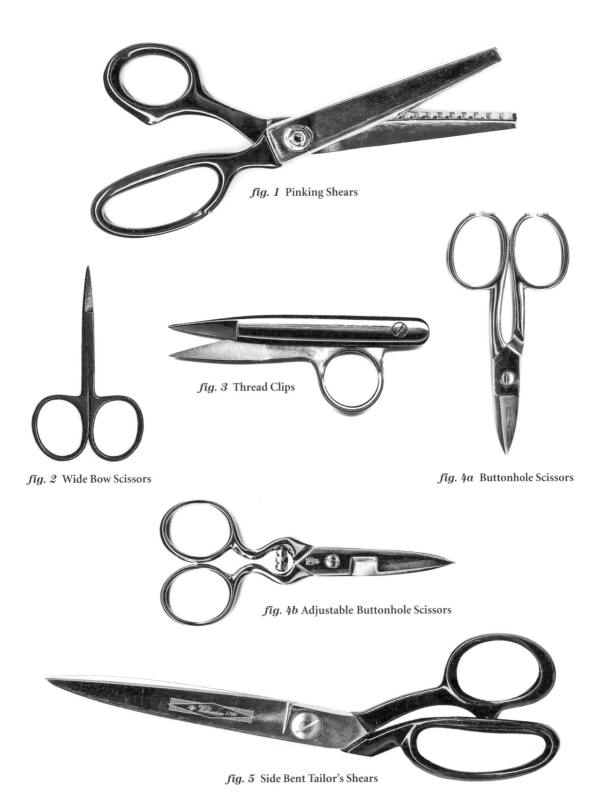

fig. 1 Pinking Shears

fig. 3 Thread Clips

fig. 2 Wide Bow Scissors

fig. 4a Buttonhole Scissors

fig. 4b Adjustable Buttonhole Scissors

fig. 5 Side Bent Tailor's Shears

THE SEWING MACHINE

The sewing machine has been around for almost 200 years[1]. These days there are some very fancy models out there doing all kinds of attractive, impressively clever computerised stitches, but all the machines we use are basic electric models from the Eighties or before. We need no more than straight, zigzag and buttonhole stitch, and even the most basic machine will offer these with a wide range of variables: stitches per inch/centimetre, width, and so on. You can pick one up for such a small sum that you might want to spend the rest on an overlocker (see p20), where it really does pay to spend as much as you can afford.

SOLVING COMMON PROBLEMS

Treat your machine well and respect the clockwork-like precision of the construction. Keep it regularly serviced and lightly oiled at all times (do not over oil as this may clog up the delicate works, and oil drips will ruin your cloth).

If you encounter a problem, it is most likely to be in the set up. Rethread the machine (this is the sewing equivalent of re-booting the computer): most machines have the same basic arrangement for thread and many have a very welcome yet discreet diagram for threading printed somewhere inside a flap or door. If this brings no joy then rethread the bobbin.

Tension is also another common problem. Check the dial (generally on the front of the machine and pictured right): the top tension is adjusted to match the bottom tension, and you should not mess with bobbin tension adjustments unless you know what you are doing. Bobbins vary from machine to machine so consult your manual (if your model is second-hand and came without a manual, it should be possible to download one).

Always test new fabrics for correct tension and stitch length: sewing on a single layer will not give you a correct assessment, so stitch through two layers as you would when project making.

It is a good idea to begin each new project with a new needle, appropriate in size and strength to the

INSIDE INFORMATION

We love a solid metal machine from a good maker and they are ridiculously cheap to buy having never become cool or collectible. On account of the weight, an older machine is unlikely to jump around at speed and will remain solid and sturdy for another 30 years if looked after properly. If at all possible, have your machine set into a firm tabletop; these can be bought new or made from an existing desk or small table with judicious use of a jigsaw.

---

[1] In 1830 French tailor Barthelemy Thimonnier nearly lost his life at the hands of enraged tailors whose livelihoods were threatened by his newfangled invention, the sewing machine. He could not at the time have known the power of what he had created. Because of him, you can sit comfortably at home, creating to your heart's content, so make him proud.

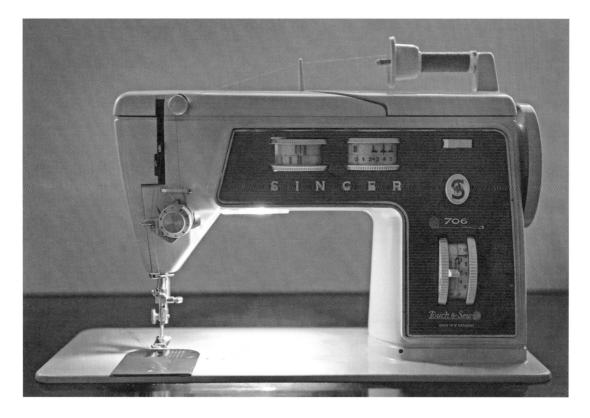

task in hand (see below). Needles are cheap and do not last forever, especially if you are sewing synthetic fabrics. A dull or over-used needle can cause snagging or puckering and at worst may bend or snap instead of making a nice tidy hole. By the way, always take the fabric and the threads out of the back of the machine to prevent unnecessary pull on the cloth or strain on the needle, which may cause it to bend or even break.

MACHINE NEEDLES

There seems to be a needle for every purpose, from the Metallica, used for sewing with delicate metallic thread, to the flighty wing needle, which has 'wings' to create wider holes in tightly woven linens. As a ground rule, match the needle size to the cloth and thread (see Size Matters, p20), and only go to the specialist alternatives if the job demands it. A few that we regularly use are listed here:

BALLPOINT Ideal to use on jersey, stretch and synthetic fabrics.

JEANS Designed for heavy-duty stitching and suitable for denim fabrics. Featuring a very sharp point and stiff shank, they are used for stitching jeans, canvas and multiple layers of fabric. Available in most sizes, we use this needle in size 14/90 for all our oilskin stitching.

TWIN-POINTED With two needles on a single shaft, this clever little needle forms parallel stitches like those running down the side of your jeans. Check that the hole in the base plate of your machine is wide enough to take the needle. In the following examples the second number indicates the distance between the two needles:

Size 11 × 2mm   Suitable for fine to medium fabrics

Size 14 × 4mm   Suitable for medium to heavy fabrics

LEATHER Specifically designed for stitching through leather, suede and vinyl, these needles have a slight cutting point to pierce the 'fabric'. Never use on woven or knit fabrics.

SIZE MATTERS

Machine needle sizes are always quoted in imperial and metric. Standard, regular-point machine needles are designed for domestic sewing machines and are used for basic stitching.

Size 10/70	Suitable for light fabrics, silk and taffeta
Size 11/80	Suitable for medium fabrics, cotton, linen and satin
Size 14/90	Suitable for medium to heavy fabrics and heavier woollens – this is an ideal in-between needle
Size 16/100	Suitable for heavy fabrics, denim, tweeds, curtain fabrics and soft furnishings
Size 18/110	Suitable for upholstery fabrics
Size 20/120	Suitable for thick denim and heavy canvas

THE OVERLOCKER

Having an overlocking machine (also known as a serger) is a real bonus and adds a professional finish to your garment. It works much like zigzag stitch on steroids; it comprehensively fastens open edges and trims excess fabric in one swift run through. It is by no means a necessity, but if you find yourself constantly sewing and finishing, you will not regret the investment. However don't buy cheap or you will spend a lifetime rethreading.

Overlockers can be used with three or four threads: the three threads are used for finishing the seam with an overcast stitch that wraps around the edge of the seam, and the fourth thread adds a running stitch to hold the seams together. Overlocking is great for stretch fabric.

INSIDE INFORMATION

When changing the threads on an overlocker you should never unthread the machine. Simply snip the threads on the reel at the back and firmly tie the new thread to the cut thread. Gently pull the threads through the machine from the machine foot.

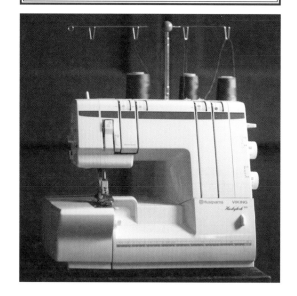

Other Useful Notions

Here are a few of the other everyday essentials that we find we cannot live without.

BAMBOO POINT TURNER

The proper tool for turning out corners: you may be tempted to use your scissors or a pencil or pen instead but this can often spell disaster, piercing through your short-lived corner. Use to 'chew' into the corner rather than to push.

THIMBLE

Protects your fingertips when hand stitching. You will either get on with using one or not. For some, they are uncomfortable, sweaty and feel constraining. We prefer the tailor's thimble with a hole in the top as this allows the finger to breathe and you can still feel the cloth, but you do have to get used to pushing the needle from the side rather than the top.

BODKIN AND THREADER

A good-quality needle threader can save hours of frustration. Cheap ones don't last; choose an all-metal version and take good care of it. A bodkin looks like a giant flat needle. It is great for threading ribbon, drawstrings and elastic, and far easier to use than a safety pin.

SEAM RIPPER

A timesaving tool for unpicking stitches. Although not really how unpicking should be done[2], it will allow you to quickly get back on track when things go wrong. Seam rippers are usually cheap and mass-produced, so replace regularly and keep a spare handy.

LOOP TURNER

This is a torturous-looking wire-and-hook implement for turning sewn tubes of bias binding, or similar, the right way round. It is ideal for making spaghetti straps or looped buttonholes, though often usurped by a humble knitting needle in practice.

MUM'S THE WORD

There are two things in the Merchant & Mills sewing kit that Mother has passed down to us: beeswax and fuller's earth.

Beeswax is traditionally used by tailors to strengthen thread when hand-sewing buttonholes: keep it by the sewing machine and pull your thread across it a couple of times before snipping off the thread end and it will be as easy as pie to get the stiff neat end through the machine needle.

Fuller's earth is naturally occurring absorbent clay that in powder form can be sprinkled onto the fingers to avoid grease marks when working on delicate fabrics.

---

[2] For those who really want to know, the correct method of unpicking is to pull the top trailing thread end until it snaps, then turn over your work and pull the now loose bobbin thread, again until it snaps.

HABERDASHERY

A PANOPLY OF SMALL THINGS

In the earliest recordings of the word, a haberdasher was simply 'a seller of various small articles of trade'. Nowadays, haberdashery has become strictly a sewing term, covering all those items we surround ourselves with. On account of our utilitarian ethos, we rarely dabble in some of the jollier products like sequins. We like rivets and industrial sash cord for our bags and, for simplicity's sake, we tend to avoid zips and buttons in dress construction. In this chapter we introduce a small sampling of haberdashery, with a little history thrown in.

THREAD

Once upon a time, thread came on lovely wooden reels with charming designs printed on round labels, top and bottom. Invariably it was made from cotton and so we called it cotton. Today though, we are more likely to be working with the ubiquitous sew-all multipurpose thread. Made from 100% polyester and slippery as silk, it resists knotting and is the professionals' choice for its strength, durability and endless range of colours. Sometimes however, you will need a specialist thread according to the cloth and nature of your project.

TYPES OF THREAD

POLYESTER THREAD Usually labelled 'sew-all' or 'all-purpose', this is the thread you will see in your local sewing shop. It has the widest range of colours and is suitable for all types of fabric. It is the first choice for nearly every non-specialist sewing task and it is ideal both for hand sewing and machine use. It is also highly resistant to unexpected knotting.

COTTON THREAD Use for light and medium-weight cotton fabrics that have little or no stretch to them. Cotton thread is essential if you want to dye the fabric. It is not as strong as sew-all thread having no elasticity, so your stitching can break if it is used on a stretchy fabric.

SILK THREAD This is the best option for fabric that has stretch to it. It has more 'give' than sew-all thread and is made for use with delicately woven, thin fabrics such as those used for lingerie.

INSIDE INFORMATION

Choose a thread colour to match the dominant colour in your fabric. If there is no dominant colour in a patterned fabric, topstitch is best avoided as it rarely works well across colours.

Always remember daylight is the best way to judge colour. If you can't find a perfect match, select a thread one or two shades darker; lighter stitching will stand out.

Although you should always use silk thread for finer silks, don't use it for chunkier or raw silks.

HEAVY-DUTY THREAD Made for sewing strong and durable stitches in particularly stiff or heavy fabrics such as strong canvas or upholstery. Jeans thread and upholstery thread will match the heavier weight of your fabric and are much better suited to the demands of these weighty cloths.

TOPSTITCHING THREAD A heavier weight thread designed to make topstitching stand out rather than look like a deep scratchy line on your project. It can look much better than standard threads on heavier fabrics where the stitching can disappear into the fabric.

PINS

Despite its tiny size, the humble pin bears a lot of responsibility in the sewing process. There is a vast array of pins made for every application from fine silk to upholstery and so much more. In general, we use dressmaking, entomology, glass-headed and toilet pins. Buy the best you can, and if you are using a specialist fabric match it to a specialist pin.

STANDARD DRESSMAKING PINS

Stainless steel pins are the most common and, for our purposes, the most useful. They are fabricated from corrosion-resistant wire that is hard to bend, allegedly, though try explaining that to a careless sewing machine. Our size of choice is 30mm × 0.6mm. For brass and mild-steel alternatives, a nickel finish is applied to ensure they remain as shiny as new pins.

Standard pins have a sharp point, but you can also find extra sharp as well as ballpoint for knitted fabrics.

GLASS-HEADED PINS

Some prefer to use glass-headed pins for all dressmaking. They are easy to find in the fabric and the large head makes them easy to handle whilst preventing them from slipping through open weave fabrics. They are heat-resistant, unlike plastic-headed pins, which quite frankly fail to earn a place in our dressmaking world.

ENTOMOLOGY PINS

Although originally intended for pinning butterflies and the like, we find these long, fine, exquisite pins are an essential workroom ally. The better versions will be enamelled and hence will not corrode to leave a mark in your fabric. This makes them first choice for very fine silks and antique fabrics, and a joy to use. Note: entomology pins often have a nylon head so be sure to remove them before pressing.

CAWKINS OR TOILET PINS

Traditionally long and strong glass-headed pins, to be used for thick layers of fabric or heavy weights like denim. They are also especially useful in curtain making.

LILLIKINS OR DUCHESSE PINS

We love these just for their name. They are the tiniest of ultra-fine, small-headed pins for fine fabrics and sheers. Indispensable for very fine appliqué and lace work.

DIPPED-HEADED PINS

These are traditionally coloured for lace making so that you can use the colours to follow the pattern. As they have finer heads than glass-headed pins, they are more accurate to place and less likely to get caught.

A WORD OF WARNING

Don't leave pins in fabric any longer than you need to as they can leave permanent holes.

Pins pictured from left to right: standard, lillikins or duchesse, dipped-headed, glass-headed, cawkins or toilet, and entomology.

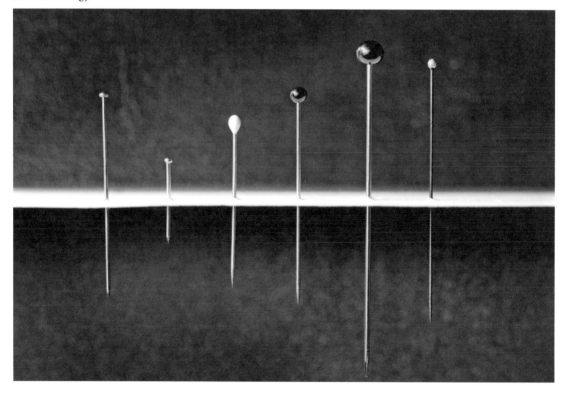

NEEDLES

Needles are, of course, at the very heart of sewing with archaeological finds uncovering truly ancient examples fashioned from animal bone. For most sewing projects we do not go far beyond the stalwart sharp. As eyes get older, the easy-thread type becomes a real friend, especially when used under the glare of a 150w bare light bulb.

SHARPS

These medium length needles are the most popular needle for hand sewing and feature a sharp point with a round eye. Much like pins, there are different qualities available, the most premium being coated with a mixture of platinum and titanium. However, the stainless steel or good old-fashioned nickel-coated varieties have yet to let us down. Needle sizes are chosen according to the fabric you are stitching:

Size 2, 3 and 4	Suitable for medium to heavy fabrics
Size 5, 6, 7, 8, 9 and 10	Suitable for light to medium fabrics
Size 11 and 12	Suitable for fine fabrics or small delicate stitching

Needles pictured from left to right: sharps, between, easy-thread, long darner, straw, mattress, darner, curved repair.

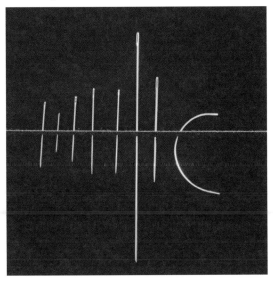

QUILTING OR BETWEENS

These needles are very short and fine with a small round eye and are the best needles for slip stitch and hemming. Their short length renders them easy to manoeuvre to create quick and even stitching, making them a favourite of the artful tailor whilst being similarly well suited to the fine art of quilting. Sizes range from 5 to 12, and we recommend starting with a size 7 or 8.

STRAWS

These are traditionally used in hat making, hence they are also known as milliner's needles. They are extra long with round eyes and are ideal for speedy tacking, basting and pleating. Straws are available in sizes 3 to 10 and should be chosen according to the demands of your cloth.

EASY-THREAD

Also known as calyx eye needles, these have a slotted eye at the top through which the thread is passed. They are specially made for people who have difficulty threading ordinary needles.

DARNERS

These are serious needles with long eyes suitable for thick thread or yarn. As the name suggests, they are the perfect choice for darning your socks and also do a good job of more industrious mending projects.

LONG DARNERS

These are more like straws and can handle not only darning but also basting and layering fabrics together.

CURVED REPAIR

This type of needle is really useful for awkward tasks as the bend puts the point right where you can find it, especially in a tight corner. It may take a little getting used to but it will be worth it.

MATTRESS

A very long needle designed to go right through a cushion or thinner mattress. We use this straight sewing needle for securing covered buttons onto our cushions.

FASTENINGS

Without fastenings, most of our clothes would be loose, floppy and more revealing than anyone is comfortable with. For the sake of simplicity in our dress patterns, we tend to avoid zips and buttons etc., but there will always come a point when two pieces of cloth need to be held together in use.

BUTTONS

There must be as many buttons in the world as grains of sand. They are vastly collectable and can make or break a sewing project. The gamut of sizes, style, materials and colours is infinite, from the standard transparent two-hole shirt number to the bespoke covered button with your own choice of cloth; they are a neat and simple way to stamp your personality

BUTTON WISE

The humble button, an ancient decorative item, only became a fastening in the fourteenth century with the addition of cord loops and eventually the buttonhole. It's hard to imagine such an inoffensive little object as controversial but both the regal French and the Victorians adorned their vestments in such quantity that they were seen as indulgent and gauche.

To this day, the Amish disallow buttons for their worldliness. Also bear in mind as you casually fasten your coat, all those who suffer from koumpounophobia, a morbid fear of buttons that leads sufferers to shiver at the very mention of the word.

on a garment. You can spend a fortune or join the ranks of charity shop raiders, liberating old dresses and coats for a nice set of buttons at a bargain price.

ZIPS

For all its popularity, the zip as we know it is only 100 years old. It's the only haberdashery item we've found that is onomatopoeic, named after the sound it makes. Choose a zip according to your cloth, pay attention to the weight and base fabric, and fit it neatly so it sits nice and flat.

HOOKS AND EYES

These are bought on a card for individual use or on a tape for corseting. They are particularly discreet and come in different strengths from ultra-fine to industrial. As well as being used for bra fastenings, they can be found on dresses and tops, on coats and as a trouser hook and bar instead of, or as well as, a button. The dressmaker will use them above a closure, such as a zip, to bring the very top together to take the stress off the fastener.

EYELETS

These are simple metal rings to seal the cloth edges of a hole for threading cord through. They often come as a set with a simple tool for inserting them and will require a bit of hammering. Always test the eyelet on surplus fabric before attacking your finished garment.

RIVETS

What would jeans be without a copper rivet? They are great for the industrial look and add extra strength to the areas of a garment that are especially stressed. Metal rivets are very easy to use on leather and for bag making, offering you the added bonus of getting the hammer out and venting some of that repressed frustration whilst achieving a neat and professional finish.

BIAS BINDING

This sewing tape is a true staple of making – a simple narrow strip of fine fabric, cut on the bias and used to trim the fabric edge. We love a spot of bias binding; a neat and simple way to finish seams, necklines and armholes. The bias cut makes it stretchy as well as fluid, ideal for binding curved edges. You can make your own or buy it off the shelf in cotton, polycotton or satin finish, to add an extra level of considered detail to anything from summer dresses to bed throws. Remember not to over-handle the tape whilst sewing as it can lose its creasing and sensitive fabric stain.

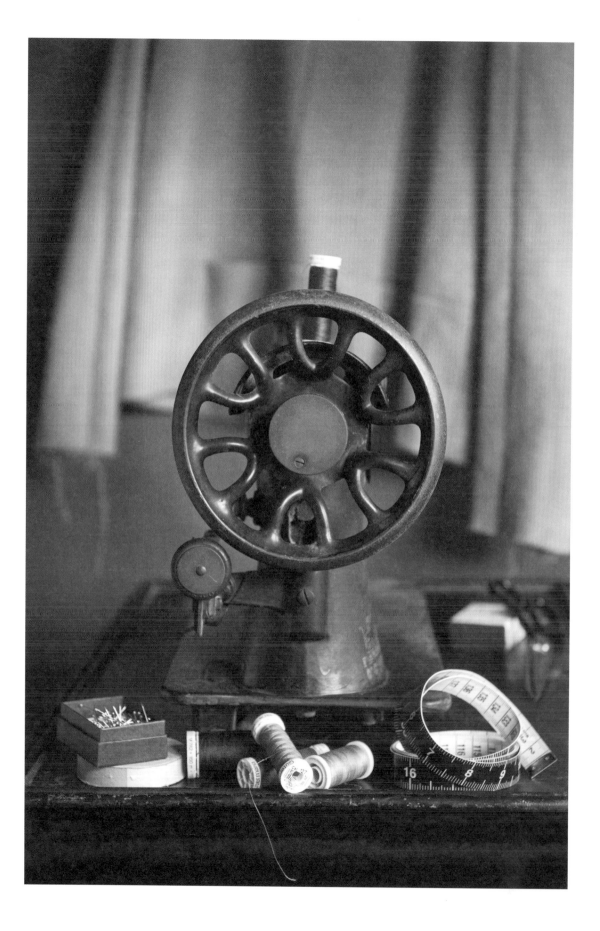

BASIC SEWING TECHNIQUES

THE INSIDE INFORMATION ON CONSTRUCTION

Sewing projects start with a piece of lovingly chosen cloth to be transformed into a three-dimensional item that we can wear, carry or use. Without an understanding of basic techniques, achieving this simple goal with any degree of aplomb would be at best haphazard. In this chapter we take a look at some basic sewing methods encountered in daily dressmaking and describe our approach to resolving common difficulties.

FORM

Starting with a jigsaw of cut cloth pieces, you will need to begin forming shape and fit. Persuading cloth to fit the human body hinges on the management of excess fabric and this is most easily done using darts or gathering. These same techniques can also be used decoratively. Much of the sculpting is done before you begin joining up the pieces, but trimming and managing the bulk from layers of cloth will come later.

DARTS

A dart is simply a wedge-shaped segment designed to accommodate curves (Fig 1). Essential to a perfect dart is ensuring that the stitches go right to the end of the dart so as not to create a bubble at its finish (Fig 2). On solid or heavier fabrics, sew right off the end of the fabric, then backstitch; with finer fabrics, leave long trailing threads when removing the cloth from the sewing machine and hand sew back into the dart stitching.

For waist darts, start in the middle, sew out to the point; then start in the middle again and sew out to the other end (Fig 3).

Large darts on solid fabrics can be snipped open to help spread and disperse the bulk (Fig 4).

Darts should be pressed really well (see Pressing Matters, p61).

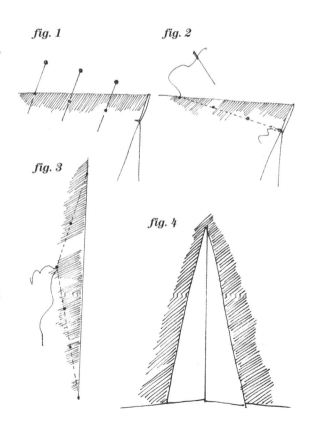

fig. 1 *fig. 2* *fig. 3* *fig. 4*

GATHERING

This is one of the simplest methods of adding detail or fit to your garment. For an even and tidy gather, set your machine to its largest straight stitch and leave long trailing threads to pull at either end of your stitching. Working inside the seam allowance, sew along the length of the intended gather, being sure to backstitch at the beginning to make one end secure. Then sew a second, parallel line from the other direction (Fig 5). Now simply take it in turns to pull gently at the end of each thread and watch your gather shrink together in nice even gathers (Fig 6).

To pin the gathered piece to its matching piece of fabric, match notches and align seams; spread and even out the gathers along the matching seam and pin together. Sew along the gathered side, making sure all the gathers lie flat as you sew. Do not press the seam open as this will flatten the gathering; instead press both seams up onto the flat (ungathered) side.

fig. 5

fig. 6

SEAMS

With the initial shape and fit prepared, you will want to start putting the pieces together. A standard seam allowance is 1.5cm so this is how far from your fabric edge your stitching should be. At the beginning of a seam start sewing a little inside the start of the seam. Sew a few stitches forward and then using the reverse stitch lever, sew back to the very beginning of the seam, then carry on sewing. This backstitch secures the thread and should be done at the beginning and end of every seam.

SEWING A PLAIN SEAM

The sewing of a seam is a fundamental sewing technique. As ever, match your thread to your cloth and sew straight (Fig 1). To practise your straight sewing, see The Calico Bag, p66. The stitch length on your machine is adjustable and as a general rule, thicker fabrics take fewer stitches per centimetre than finer ones. In industry larger stitches are used as an economy, but as a home sewer you are free to make these choices yourself. Press your seams open (see Pressing Matters, p61) and finish the seam allowance edges as necessary (see Finishing Seam Allowance Edges, opposite).

fig. 1

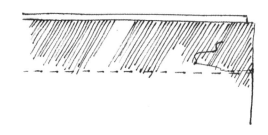

TWO SPECIAL SEAMS

Featured below are two encased seams that you might find useful; these do not require the raw seam edges to be finished.

RUN AND FELL

This seam is only suitable for densely woven, non-fray fabrics and is especially suitable for boiled or felted wool. You will need to be pretty nifty at topstitching to do this well. Sew together a plain seam on the right side of the garment. Trim off the under seam. Lay the top seam over and edge stitch down (Fig 2). For a nice detail on bags, etc., try pinking the top seam before stitching down (Fig 3).

fig. 2

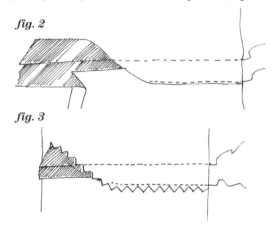

fig. 3

FRENCH SEAM

You will often find this seam on patterns that use very fine fabrics, for example lingerie or soft furnishings.

Sew together a plain seam on the right side of the garment, taking approximately a 9mm seam allowance. Trim the seam down (Fig 4). Turn the garment to the wrong side so that the raw edges of the first seam are encased.

fig. 4

With the seam on the edge, sew another seam about 6mm from the folded edge (Fig 5). Press at each stage (Fig 6).

fig. 5

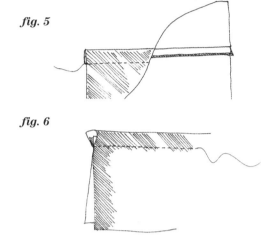

fig. 6

FINISHES ON A STANDARD SEAM

Standard seams often require finishing for many reasons: to stabilise fraying fabrics, to reduce bulk, and to create a neat and professional finish to your stitched garment.

FINISHING SEAM ALLOWANCE EDGES

ZIGZAG This does a good job of preventing the fabric edge from fraying. Don't zigzag on the very edge of the seam, as this will inevitably cause the seam to pucker.

fig. 7

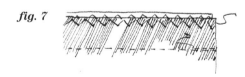

OVERLOCKING If you are lucky enough to have an overlocker, you can spend some time preventing frayed edges before you go on to start your seams. The overlocker has a blade to trim the cloth edge as you sew but does not go around corners like zigzag can. Stretchy fabrics such as jersey are best overlocked after the seam has been sewn, as the seam edges work better overlocked together (Fig 8).

fig. 8

PINKING SHEARS The charactcristic zigzag cdgcs left behind by pinking shears are a cunning and simple way to combat fraying and present a lovely flat finish (Fig 9). This finish is only suitable for tightly woven fabrics and should not be used on knits or heavier wool fabrics.

fig. 9

TRIMMING SEAMS

The correct trimming of seams to get rid of excess bulk is essential for all areas of dressmaking. This is especially important around necklines and underarms, which will need to be snipped or notched to spread or contract the fabric. Snip an internal curve (Fig 10) but notch out on an external curve (Fig 11).

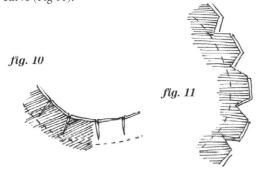

fig. 10

fig. 11

Corners sewn inside out will need to be trimmed off to create a nice flat seam when the garment is turned through to the right side (Fig 12).

Bulky seams with a facing can be trimmed at different levels on each side so that the unwanted bulk is staggered for a flatter finish (Fig 13).

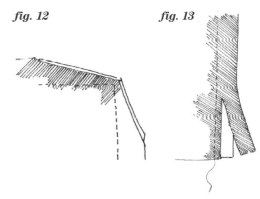

fig. 12   *fig. 13*

TOPSTITCH

Topstitching is an extra line of stitching made parallel to the seam on the right side of the fabric for definition. Some fabrics do not take kindly to topstitching so do some trials on a spare piece of your garment fabric. If you are in doubt do not topstitch, as bad topstitching can ruin a good project.

Generally avoid topstitching thick woollens and any fabrics with a deep pile such as velvet, as topstitch will just get swallowed up on these. Domestic sewing machines don't cope very well with bulky seams on thick fabrics; so however good you are at topstitching, expect to be disappointed here. However, stable fabrics with a fairly tight weave such as linen and cotton – which includes everything from drill to oilskin – topstitch very well.

It is usually better to fold your seams together to one side to topstitch through both at once for a more solid finish (Fig 14).

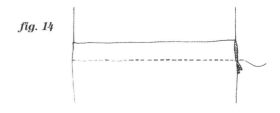

fig. 14

EDGE STITCHING

Edge stitching is a line of stitching made directly next to the seam line. We like a spot of edge stitching as it can make seams look very neat and professional. It is always best to open and flatten your seams really well and give them a good roll first, as this will help the seam sit right at the very edge exactly where you want it to be (Fig 15). Sew right at the very edge of the finished seam and around the corners. Slow down and turn the machine wheel by hand for ultimate accuracy.

fig. 15

NECK FACINGS

We often recommend an interfaced lining fabric for a neck facing as it will add much less bulk than your dress cloth and so lay nice and flat. We like to use under stitching to hold facings inside the garment as it is especially neat and tidy (Fig 16). On the curve of the neck you will need to snip into the seams to relieve the tension of the curve (see Fig 10, opposite).

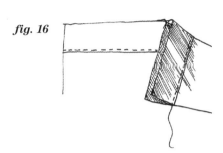

fig. 16

EASE

This is a way to add a subtle fullness and create a tailored finish by drawing threads of the fabric together in a fine, gentle gather; the squashed up fabric is pinned to its matching pattern piece and the gather disperses in the sewing. Some vintage patterns have a lot of ease especially on the back shoulder seam and around the bust where a little extra fabric is added in without interrupting the style.

SET-IN SLEEVES

The traditional way to set in a fitted sleeve makes textbook use of ease. You will need to lightly gather cloth into the top of the sleeve head to give a much better fit. This is most difficult to do on fine, tightly woven fabrics and easiest on loose-weave woollens.

Using the largest straight stitch on your sewing machine, sew a line of stitching just inside the seam allowance of your sleeve (Fig 1). Gently gather (Fig 2).

With the sleeve the right side out and the garment inside out, offer up the sleeve to the armhole (Fig 3). First pin together the notches on the sleeve, armhole and shoulder. Spread the ease between these notches. Then pin the whole sleeve in place making sure that the ease has not made any gathers on the sewing line (Fig 4). Tack in place before sewing (Fig 5).

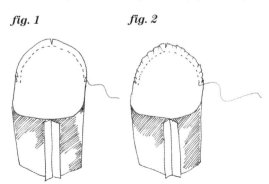

fig. 1 *fig. 2*

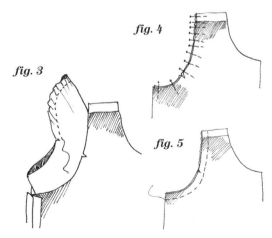

fig. 3 *fig. 4* *fig. 5*

CLOSURES

There are endless ways to fasten a garment in place on your body. The most common are zips and buttons, which we look at in some depth below. For an overview of some other fastenings, see Haberdashery, pp26–27.

MACHINING BUTTONHOLES

Nearly all sewing machines – apart from the very, very old or the absurdly cheap – will have a dedicated buttonhole function. You need to take special care to make your buttonholes straight and to the same length. Don't spoil your project with sloppy buttonholes.

The position and length of the buttonholes should be accurately marked on your cloth with tailor's tacks or chalked dots according to your pattern (Fig 1). Joining the marks together will show you the correct length and a neat bar at either end will mark the position of the end bars: make sure you have a nice capital 'I' with a clear top and bottom bar before you start sewing (Fig 2).

fig. 1   *fig. 2*

Some machines are able to automate the buttonhole process with presets, so you can simply follow the instructions on your sewing machine. If you are lacking the buttonhole option, a neat job can also be achieved manually (Fig 3). Once your stitching is in place, use buttonhole scissors to snip the fabric inside to create the hole.

fig. 3

SEWING ON A BUTTON

Although this is a simple operation, there is a correct way to do it. Buttons cannot be sewn tightly to your fabric, as they need room beneath to accommodate the buttonhole layer, so you need to create a shank, like a short stalk.

Mark the position of the buttonhole with two crossed pins (Fig 4). Centre the button over the pins and sew it on. Remove the pins. Create the shank by winding your thread tightly around the threads 6–8 times (Fig 5). Pass the needle through the shank several times and finally secure your thread through the stitching on the reverse of the cloth (Fig 6).

fig. 4   *fig. 5*   *fig. 6*

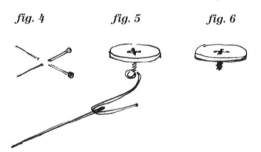

SETTING IN A ZIP

There are two basic ways of setting in a zip: centred and lapped. Each method should conceal the zip but the lapped zip is better suited to cushions and soft furnishings. For dressmaking, choose the method that best suits the style of garment you are making, for example a lapped zip might work better on a skirt or side-seamed trousers, whereas a centred zip is perfect for the back seam of a dress.

THE CENTRED ZIP

Following the notches on the pattern, loosely close the seam where the zip will go. Using the largest straight stitch on your sewing machine, sew to the notch that marks the bottom of the zip opening. Adjust the stitch length to a standard size, secure firmly with a backstitch and sew along the remainder of the seam, beyond the zip's position (Fig 7).

Place your zip face down onto the loosely sewn seam. Pin one side of the zip to the seam allowance only and tack into place. Start sewing from the bottom and keep your stitching close to the teeth of the zip (Fig 8). Repeat for the other side (Fig 9).

Turn the cloth over and starting from the bottom topstitch each side of the zip about 1cm from the seam. Join up at the bottom with a short line of horizontal stitching with a line of reverse stitch for extra strength (Fig 10). Unpick the large stitches that hold the zipped seam together.

LAPPED ZIP

When setting a lapped zip into a side seam, make sure the lapped side is in the front of the garment and the underlap is on the back. Sew the seam together up to

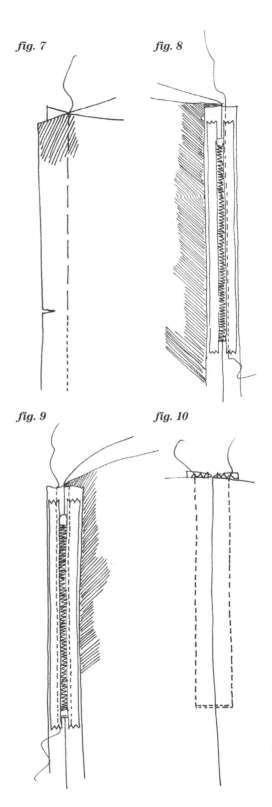

fig. 7 fig. 8

fig. 9 fig. 10

INSIDE INFORMATION

Position your zip so that the cloth tape sits about 5mm from the top edge of your fabric, so that the actual zip begins about 2.5cm from the top.

A bespoke zipper foot is a common accessory for most sewing machines and it will allow you to sew as close to the edge of the zip's teeth as possible.

the opening for the zip. Lay your zip against the seam that is to be lapped (the underlap). Starting from the bottom, pin then sew the zip on 4mm–5mm from the edge of the seam allowance (Fig 11).

Turn the garment over to the right side and fold the seam allowance down to the edge of the zip. Edge stitch along the zip, again working from the bottom up (Fig 12).

Turning back over to the wrong side, pin and sew the other side of the zip to the seam allowance, this time lining them up (Fig 13).

Turn over to the right side again. You will see that a natural fold has been made and the overlap has been created. Pin or tack the edge of the overlap to just cover the underlap. This edge will be in line with the seam below (Fig 14). Now topstitch around the overlap, starting at the bottom where the previous edge stitching finished. Sew along the bottom and up the side taking a 1cm seam allowance (Fig 15).

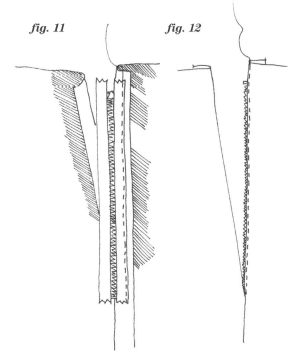

fig. 11   fig. 12

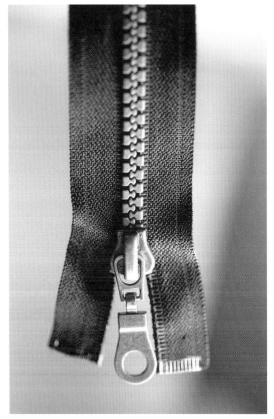

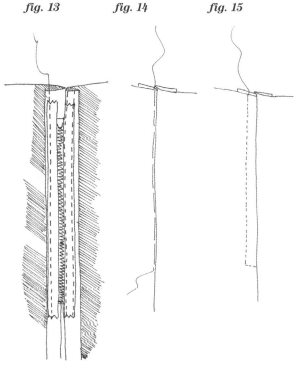

fig. 13   fig. 14   fig. 15

DRESSMAKING HEMS

Hems are one of the most important elements of good dressmaking. A hem should look and hang perfectly. The depth of a hem will depend on the thickness of your cloth; as a rule of thumb, thicker fabrics will need a deeper hem. Hand or machine finishes work well for different tasks and the choice will usually be obvious.

SLIP STITCHED HEM

Turn up your hem and press in place along the bottom edge (see Pressing Matters, p62). Turn under the edge of the hem and once you have determined your fold, use a betweens needle to pick up a stitch from the inside of your folded edge. If this edge is zigzagged, pick a stitch from the sewn thread, then catch a thread from the body of the garment. Creating a stitch around 1cm long, carry on forward taking a stitch and a thread from each side (Fig 1). Don't make the stitches too long or the hem will catch when putting the garment on.

fig. 1

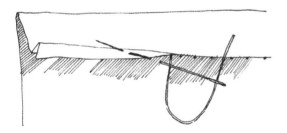

FULL HEM

If you have a circular hem, the circumference of the bottom will be larger than the turned up finished hem. On light or fine fabrics, we suggest you take a very small hem so that the difference, too, is very small and can be eased in. On chunky woollens, the hem can be easily shrunk to fit. To do this, measure the hem, turn up and pin into place, then gently steam using a damp pressing cloth to let it shrink to fit.

Alternatively, you can use a running stitch that can be very slightly tautened to take up the minor excess before steaming (Fig 2).

fig. 2

Press to finish, pressing only the bottom edge of the hem to a nice sharp line, so that the inside hemline does not show through to the front. Use a clapper on woollen fabrics (see p60).

BOUND HEMS

Hems finished with bias binding can look very neat, especially on an unlined coat or jacket. They can also work well to reduce bulk on garments made from thicker fabric. Do be aware that binding will behave differently to your garment fabric. Be especially careful not to stretch your hem as you put the binding on.

HAND-FINISHED HEMS

As dressmakers, we can hand-finish hems for that statement of pure craftsmanship that is only found on couture garments, so don't be afraid to show off your skills. Finishing by hand can be immensely satisfying at the end of your sewing project. It brings a beautiful final touch and is well suited to all fabrics, but is especially essential on wool, thicker fabrics and cloth with a deep pile.

Open out the fold along one edge of the bias binding and sew to the edge of the garment with right sides facing (Fig 3). With the binding attached, turn up the hem of the garment to the desired length and slip stitch the still folded top edge of the binding to the inside of your garment (Fig 4).

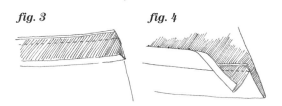

fig. 3   *fig. 4*

TOPSTITCHED HEMS

Many fabrics and garment styles really benefit from topstitch, which can add detail and finesse to the design. Turn up the hem allowance and turn under the edge of the folded hem. Press into place. Take your time when sewing to keep your topstitching lovely and straight, especially when sewing over seams. Press again after sewing to set the stitching down.

To work two lines of topstitching, use a twin-pointed needle (see p19) for perfectly parallel stitched lines.

HAND STITCHING FOR SOFT FURNISHINGS

Hand stitching is the backbone of soft furnishings. The best curtains, blinds and cushions will always be hand sewn for accuracy and lightness of touch. Mastering a few simple stitches will enable you to produce visibly superior furnishings for your home.

SLIP STITCH

This stitch is used to bring two folded edges together. It is very commonly used especially in soft furnishings. Bring the needle out from just under the fold along one edge, and working from right to left insert the needle into the other folded edge exactly opposite the first stitch, once again just beneath the edge (Fig 1). Draw the two edges together gently but firmly. Continue working forward, continuing to take a stitch from just under the edge of each fold (Fig 2).

HERRINGBONE STITCH

This is a strong crisscross stitch used on the hems of curtains and blinds. Work from left to right. With your fabric edge folded into place and inserting the needle into the hem from right to left, pick up a few threads of fabric. Pass over the edge of the hem and insert the needle into the garment, from right to left, taking a similar number of threads. Repeat along the length of your hem to produce a lovely crisscross stitch (Fig 3).

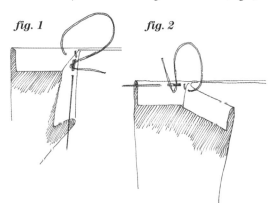

fig. 1   *fig. 2*

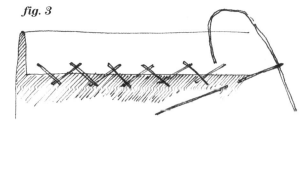

fig. 3

STAB STITCH

This is a tiny invisible stitch made on the right side of the cloth, often used for hems of blinds. Insert the needle at right angles to the fabric (Fig 4) and stab through from front to back and vice versa with the longer stitch on the underside.

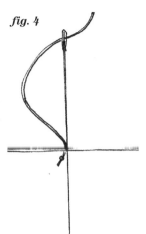

fig. 4

CATCH STITCH

Not a strong stitch, but often used on curtains and blinds, and you may also find this stitch hidden on lined garments and used to secure interfacings. Working from right to left, take up a few threads of the hem, then pass the needle diagonally over the hem and take a few threads from the surface of the garment; repeat all the way along (Fig 5). The stitches should be invisible on the right side.

fig. 5

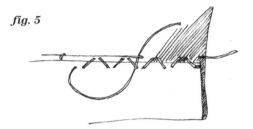

INTERFACINGS

Some areas of your garment do not want to be floppy. Interfacings are there to stiffen your fabric and give a more solid, neat and crisp finish. There seem to be hundreds of woven, bonded or knitted interfacings out there, each designed for appropriate pairing with your cloth.
We focus on fusible interfacings as they are generally the choice of modern dressmakers.
This convenient solution bypasses many hours of intensive attaching as it simply glues to the fabric under a hot iron and often stiffens when pressed. The best way to make sure your interfacing is a good match is to buy it at the same time as the fabric, taking advice from the retailer.

CHOOSING AND USING

The key to interfacings is to choose the right weight for the fabric. Lightweight interfacings are best suited to dresses, tops and shirts; medium-weight is ideal for jackets; and the heavier weights are used for coats. Knitted interfacings are available for stretch fabrics. If in doubt, we recommend that you err on the side of the lighter weights, as a too heavy choice will look unnaturally stiff and cause your garment to stand away from the body. No one wants a shirt that looks like it's made of hardboard!

Handle fusible interfacings with care so as not to stretch the garment piece as you iron it on. Start by laying out your cut fabric piece face down on your sturdy ironing board. (Take special care not to distort the cloth, especially if it is a small or awkwardly shaped piece.) Lay the corresponding pattern piece on top to ensure the shape matches perfectly and then remove it without disturbing the garment piece. Place your pre-cut fusible interfacing on top with its glue-side down and press: lift the iron and place it back down rather than pushing it along.

When using heavier weight fabric and interfacings, you should trim the seam allowance off the fusible interfacing and let it butt up to your final sewing line. Make sure it is nicely stuck down as you will not be sewing through it. This will reduce bulk at the seam.

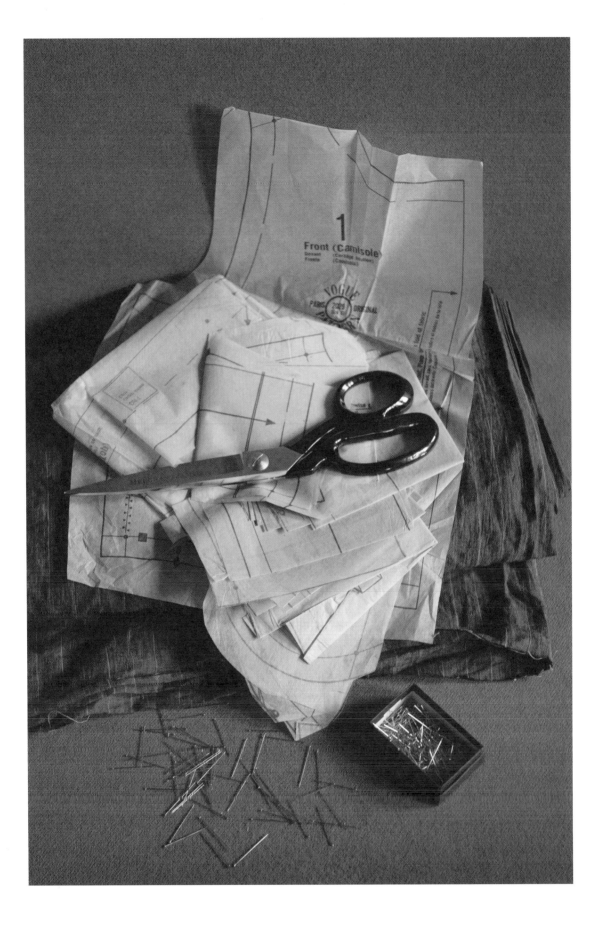

Patterns

YOUR TEMPLATE FOR MAKING

Thanks to Ebenezer Butterick of Sterling, Massachusetts, graded paper patterns have been rustling their way across our fabrics for nearly 150 years[1]. Today's multi-size tissue paper patterns have a lot going for them if used properly. In the fashion industry, production patterns are made from a heavier brown card, in single sizes. These are the patterns we use for our daily making and that we sell to our customers. In this chapter we guide you through understanding patterns, using paper or card patterns, and making basic pattern alterations for the very best fit.

UNDERSTANDING PATTERNS

Dressmaking patterns can be daunting but once you get to grips with the language, they do have all the information you need for use. Each pattern piece is marked with the number of pieces to be cut – normally one or two – and will also advise if a matching piece of interlining should be cut. Fabric is fluid whereas card and paper are not, so keep a constant eye out for rucks and distortion.

FABRIC LAYOUT

Patterns will give you layouts for different widths of fabric, so choose the one that suits. Some patterns will have a nap layout, which is important for fabrics prone to shading, such as velvet. The instructions will tell you whether a given pattern piece is to be used print side up or face down so pay attention!

We always prefer to cut out with all our pieces facing the same direction on the fabric. This may use more cloth but bypasses those annoying panel mismatches arising from hidden nap that has a very slight difference in direction; even on non-pile fabric, this can lead to a shading effect on the final garment.

PATTERN MARKINGS

These are commonly called transfer markings because you will need to transfer many of them from your pattern to your cloth.

CUTTING LINE The edge of the pattern and the place to cut!

SEAM ALLOWANCE Shown on all patterns with a long broken line and usually the standard 1.5cm. Study the pattern pieces to see if this seam allowance changes anywhere, such as the underarm for example.

NOTCHES These are for matching seams, and they are essential for matching up your pieces correctly, particularly where there is ease in the seam, such as the sleeve head.

---

[1] Initially Butterick produced his patterns on heavy cardboard for rigidity but as a canny businessman, he moved to foldable paper for ease of distribution. Early patterns came without markings and in one mid size for the experienced seamstress to grade and adapt to her shape, and the printed-paper versions first appeared in 1948.

THE GRAIN LINE This line needs to be matched up to the grain direction of the fabric. The grain follows the selvedge edge so the grain line needs to run parallel to this. Note that some patterns will be bias cut and the grain line will run across the grain. Some neck yokes will run at a right angle to the grain. ⟶▷

DARTS AND DOTS These are markings that show the position of the darts or other details, such as pockets. They need to be accurately and clearly marked with tailor's tacks (see opposite) or chalk.

BUTTONHOLES These must be marked clearly with tailor's tacks or chalk. ⊢———⊣

LENGTHEN AND SHORTEN LINES These two parallel lines are guide lines to where you can alter the garment length. (You cannot alter everywhere as this will affect the style or fit of the pattern.) ═══════

FOLD LINES These are marked on half pattern pieces, denoting where to position at the fold of your cloth. As they are only half the final shape it is most important you position these pattern pieces the right way up.

USING PATTERNS

Whether you prefer to work with paper or card patterns, each type will lead to similar results but requires quite different techniques in use, as described below.

WORKING WITH PAPER PATTERNS

These are printed on tissue paper as one giant sheet for simpler designs, or more often, a set of sheets. They are provided in A5 envelopes with fabulous, full-colour drawings of the finished garment and are complete with a glossary and instructions, including a key to the pattern markings. The main challenge is to identify the correct line for your desired size and then to meticulously follow it with your sharp, paper scissors.

In use, the pattern pieces are pinned to your cloth and cut around. Here are our top tips for working with paper patterns:

☞ Iron your paper pattern before cutting out to remove factory fold lines.

☞ Cut out pattern pieces carefully and accurately.

☞ Press your fabric at the outset; it doesn't take long and will speed things up later.

☞ Lay fabric out flat; if the pattern requires you to fold your cloth in half, make sure you do so with the right sides facing.

☞ Pin the pattern to the cloth so that the pins align with the fabric edge, keeping both pattern and cloth flat, even and undistorted.

☞ After cutting out your cloth, mark all the darts and other garment details with tailor's tacks.

☞ Once any markings have been transferred, unpin the pattern pieces straight away as handling with pins in may rip the tissue.

MARKING TAILOR'S TACKS

Tailor's tacks are simply for marking. They are made through the tissue pattern and fabric layer(s) before unpinning the pattern piece. Use a knotted double thread to make several long loops through each pattern dot that needs to be marked (Fig 1).

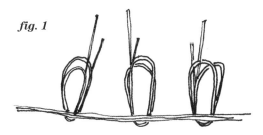

fig. 1

FOR SINGLE LAYER FABRIC Snip the top of the loops and very gently lift off your paper pattern.

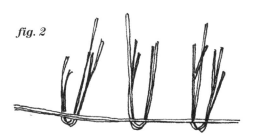

fig. 2

FOR FOLDED FABRIC Gently start to separate the two layers of fabric. As you reach the tailor's tack, snip it in half so that you have a half tack on both pieces of cloth.

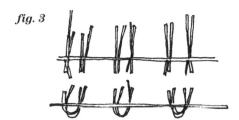

fig. 3

WORKING WITH CARD PATTERNS

We like card patterns as they behave better in use and can be used time and time again. They are more rigid and can be persuaded to lie perfectly still and flat. Our patterns are supplied in individual sizes and are already cut into a collection of pieces. They do not need to be pinned out but instead are weighted down onto the fabric with pattern weights (or handy this of beans) and marked around with tailor's chalk. All notches are snipped and all internal details such as darts or pockets are drilled out with holes ready to be marked with chalk.

- ☞ If your card pattern arrives in a roll, unfurl and roll in the reverse direction to regain its flatness.
- ☞ Press your fabric at the outset; it doesn't take long and will speed things up later.
- ☞ Carefully chalk all the way around the pattern as you would a stencil, using a sharp tailor's chalk in a contrasting colour. Use the fingers of your spare hand to flatten down the edge of the pattern as you chalk – this will keep the marking accurate.
- ☞ Mark all notches with a snip into the seam and mark all details such as darts with tailor's chalk.
- ☞ When working on folded cloth, remember to pin the layers together and mark the underneath cloth too.

CUTTING OUT CLOTH

Use good light and take your time; accuracy is more important than speed. Try not to lift the fabric as you are cutting.

We use side bent scissors, which are specifically designed to overcome the problem of lifting fabric; in use the bottom blade stays parallel to the tabletop (or floor) whilst the upper blade moves to do the cutting.

BASIC DRESS PATTERN ALTERATIONS

Bodies come in all shapes and sizes and it really is quite amazing that a few pieces of paper can be manipulated to fit anybody at all. If you find yourself amongst the majority of us who were supplied with non-standard sized bodies, you will need to make some adjustments to your patterns. Learning some basic techniques for manipulating standard patterns will open the door to a much better fitting self-made wardrobe.

TOILES

A toile is a working mock up of the final garment made from a cheaper fabric to check fit and styling details, and it informs the maker where to make changes. We recommend using calico for toile making; this comes in many different weights to allow for a good match to the cloth you are planning to use. However, any similar weight cloth to your intended cloth can be pressed into service for the toile.

When we create a new design for our company we will make many toiles. We will draw all over them and cut and unpick at them to give us what we want. We then transfer these changes to our pattern and alter it accordingly. At each stage, we make a new pattern, which allows us to always have an unchanged original as well as a card story of the design's development. Don't be alarmed; alterations to an existing pattern are considerably less daunting than developing a pattern from scratch. However, because things can get complicated, we strongly advise you to trace off your original pattern onto craft paper at the outset, so you can return to it should things go horribly wrong.

Even with a toile, it is often difficult to see exactly how the alteration can be successfully made on the final pattern. In the pages that follow, we explain a few simple adjustments that can be made to your pattern pieces.

BEFORE YOU BEGIN

While making pattern amendments may seem like a lot of hard work, rest assured that your industry will be rewarded, as you will achieve a more bespoke and professional look to your finished garments. The more you do it, the better you will become until you cannot imagine leaving a pattern alone! However, there are a few things you need to be aware of before you get underway with the pattern adjustments outlined on pp45–48.

IMPORTANT

☞ Do not tamper with the centre front line, as this will affect the balance of the whole garment.

☞ All alterations will need to be carried through to neighbouring pattern pieces.

☞ Adjustments are made by adding in or taking out volume at the same point on both pieces.

☞ Backing paper is necessary to stick your altered pattern to; you can buy all kinds of pattern paper but craft paper or even newspaper will do the job.

☞ In all diagrams on pp45–48, the shaded areas mark either the pieces that will move or where the alteration occurs.

BLEND

Blend in your reshaping to form a smooth sewing line. This must be done on all seams and on darts. Always alter from the sewing line not the cutting line. Once you are happy with the alteration, draw on a new seam allowance.

Blending darts After the alterations and before trimming away the backing paper, fold and pin the darts along their sewing line. Fold the darts in the direction indicated in the pattern instructions and draw smoothly along the sewing line (Fig 1). Add on the seam allowance and trim back to the cutting line. This will give you the familiar point shapes to the dart cutting line (Fig 2).

fig. 1   *fig. 2*

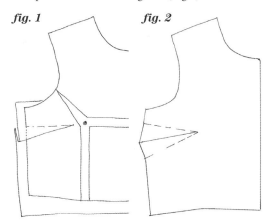

PATTERN ADJUSTMENT TOOL KIT

There are just a few essentials you will need:

- A sharp pencil
- Transparent grading rulers or triangle; a French curve also helps (see above right)
- Backing paper
- Sticky tape – as tape can yellow and become brittle over time, the softer translucent tape is the best
- Paper scissors

BUST DART POSITION

Bust alterations are amongst the most common. When you think of how many bra and cup size combinations there are, it's hardly surprising.

INSIDE INFORMATION

The French curve is a wonderful object for altering patterns. The curve can be angled and moved around to find the perfect line. Choose a transparent one with centimetre markings on the curve.

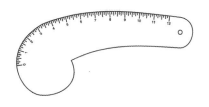

FOR A FULL BUST

Mark the position of your actual bust with a dot. Draw lines through the dart to the dot as follows: (1) at a right angle from the centre front to the dot; (2) from the armhole notch to the dot; (3) from the waist to the dot parallel to the centre front (Fig 3). Cut the dart line up to the dot but do not cut through. Cut from the waist to the dot. Cut from the centre to the dot. Cut from the armhole notch to the dot.

fig. 3

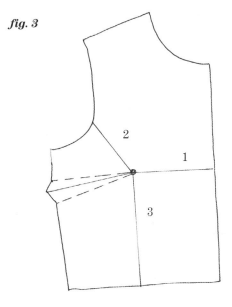

Spread the underarm out and across. The dart will open up as you do this. Open up the side waist piece; the dart will open up some more. Move the bottom centre front piece down and to the same level. Tape the pattern piece down onto backing paper (Fig 4).

Re-mark the dot in the centre of the moved pieces. Re-mark the dart point about 2.5cm away from the dot and draw in the new dart. Blend in the dart and seams (Fig 5).

Draw in a new dart about 2cm away from the new bust dot. Blend in the dart and seams (Fig 6).

FOR A HIGH OR LOW BUST

This type of alteration is particularly useful for vintage patterns, which always seem to have an incredibly high bust.

Mark the position of your actual bust with a dot. Draw a box around the dart 1cm wider on either side (Fig 7). Cut out this box and move it up or down to alter the position of the dart (Fig 8a and Fig 8b). Tape the pattern piece down onto the pattern and backing paper.

fig. 4   *fig. 5*

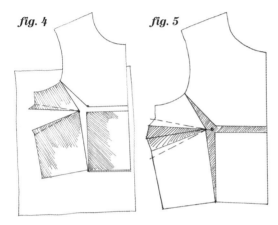

fig. 7

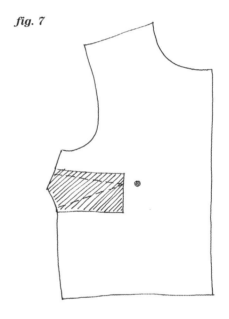

FOR A SMALL BUST

This is the same principle as adjusting for a full bust but instead of opening up the pieces you will overlap them.

Draw lines through the dart to the dot following Fig 3 above. Cut the dart line up to the dot but do not cut through. Cut from the waist to the dot. Cut from the centre to the dot. Cut from the armhole notch to the dot. Close up the dart. This will force the underarm section and the side waist piece to rise and close. Tape the pattern piece down onto backing paper. Re-mark the bust dot in the centre of the overlapped pieces.

fig. 6

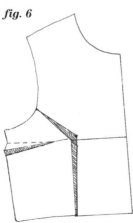

fig. 8a   *fig. 8b*

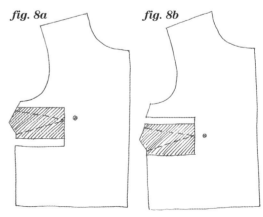

GAPING ARMHOLE

The gaping armhole is a common problem that we encounter. Removing cloth to change the angle of the shoulder seam rectifies this. If it is serious, you may need to put a small dart in the armhole.

Lift out the excess through the front shoulder seam (Fig 9). Fold back the seam allowance on the shoulder seams and blend the two seams together to make a smooth line (Fig 10).

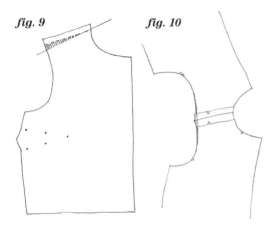

fig. 9   *fig. 10*

LARGE BACK

Adding in a little to the armhole seam and the side seam will fix this. Make sure that you add on the same amount to the side sleeve seam (Fig 12).

fig. 12

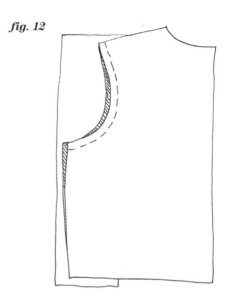

SMALL BACK

Taking out a little from the armhole and a little off the side seam is a simple resolve. Make sure that you take off the same amount from the side sleeve seam (Fig 11).

fig. 11

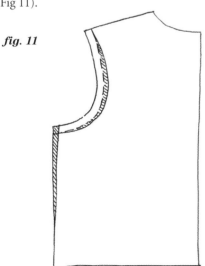

FULL UPPER ARM

This can be a particular problem for older women. Before you start, check the amount of ease in your sleeve head. To do this, measure the armhole minus seam allowances and compare it to the sleeve head measurement, again minus seam allowances. The difference between the two measurements is your ease.

Draw a line across the sleeve about 2cm above the notch lines and at a right angle to the grain line. Draw another line about 2cm below the underarm, again at a right angle to the grain line. Divide the area between the marked lines into three equal parts. Cut out the two outside pieces, leaving the middle section in place (Fig 13, p48). Move the two cut out outside pieces away from the middle section to equal the extra width needed. Blend in with the top and side seams (Fig 14, p48).

fig. 13

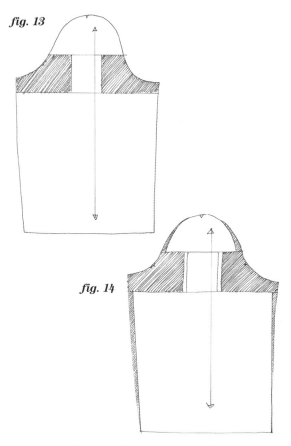

fig. 14

Now alter the bodice pieces to match. Measure the new sleeve head and check against the arms both front and back. Take off the ease allowance. There will be a small amount of adjustment needed to the shoulders and side seams (Fig 15). Keep the alteration to the shoulder smaller.

fig. 15

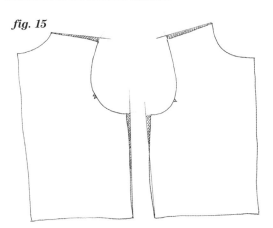

BIG TUMMY

Raise the stitching line on the centre front waist by up to 1cm and then blend in the new stitching line with the darts (Fig 16). Add in up to 1.5cm into the front side seam, and, to keep the waist measurement the same, take off the same amount from the back side seam.

fig. 16

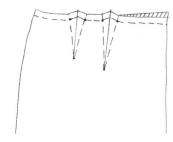

EMPTY TUMMY

Reduce the size of the darts. Take the difference of the original larger dart minus the new smaller darts off the side seam (Fig 17).

fig. 17

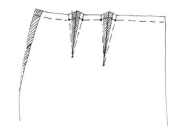

SWAY BACK

This is more common that one would think and will affect the way a centre back zip sits.

Lower the waistline from the centre back seam by up to 2cm. Blend in the darts and stitching lines (Fig 18).

fig. 18

CLOTH

THE BEAUTIFUL RAW MATERIAL

Before embarking on our heady voyage through a sea of cloth, please bear in mind that we give most attention to the fabrics we use day in and day out. A further caveat for all you colourful souls out there is that our middle name is 'drab', which the dictionary defines primarily as 'dull'. That it is to say, we lean towards the darker, more muted end of the spectrum for much of our making and are particularly alarmed by bright primary colours. This is a personal choice and should not be seen as a directive. It is important to express your own character with everything you make; there is no right or wrong.

CHOOSING FABRICS

Your fabric stash can say more about your true style than your wardrobe does. A fabric buy is instinctive and free from fleeting fashions. You may find that you always buy the same types of fabric: they are what you love. Fabric is where the home dressmaker has the edge: sew to have something that is uniquely yours.

Our preference is for natural fabrics; we know we can rely on wool, cotton, linen or silk to perform predictably each time we pick them up. These cloths are particularly well suited to our ways of working. Our fabric choices offer plenty of opportunity to experiment and master new skills.

Remember the adage 'you can't make a silk purse

The Original
MERCHANT & MILLS
DRAPER

MOTHER SAYS: 'BUY THE MOST EXPENSIVE FABRIC YOU CAN AFFORD.'

out of a sow's ear,' nevertheless, you might treat your dog with one. There are cloths that are clearly suited to certain garments. Cloth is tactile, sensuous and flowing, so let your fingers do the research.

WOOL

We love a sumptuous thick wool. Just like its lighter cousins, wool will retain its shape and throw off wrinkles with its natural stretch and elasticity that flexes with the body. It will last for years and keep you cosy when you need it most. Wool is very easy for the dressmaker to use being considerably more obedient than the animal it came from. To top it all, it manages to be relaxed and comfortable but always remains smart, lending itself to simple styles that allow the fabric to revel in its own glory.

WOOLLENS

By woollens, we mean all those delicious cloths that are pure wool, have a luxurious feel and a consistently beautiful handle. A nice dense woollen cloth is quite rigid yet soft to the touch. It comes in many weights and is extremely versatile. Be wary though as thick fabric can add bulk, so choose tailored styles.

Before buying wool with a pile, do your own

bobble test: rub your fingers over the fabric rapidly to see whether it either bobbles or stretches; if it does, quietly walk away.

When using any thick fabric, avoid thick facings and choose an interfaced lining instead.

TWEED

Rustic yet smart, coarse or fine, tweed always has an air of quality. It uses shorter wool fibres in its manufacture where the yarns have already been twisted from two or more colours before weaving. Harris and Donegal tweeds are traditionally seen in a variety of flecks, herringbone and checks, and the flexible rougher weave conjures up those Hebridean and Irish landscapes and the hardy sheep that gave their fleeces for their creation. Tweed was originally considered tough and heavy, just right for Plus Fours and a spot of hunting, shooting and fishing.

Typically it is a durable fabric with body, depth and characteristic bounce, which can be tamed with tailored and fitted detailing. Be aware when making up that tweed fabric is particularly prone to fraying.

SUPERFINE SUITING

A worsted wool cloth with light weight and a much higher yarn count, it tends to be reassuringly expensive, flow like silk and have a soft feel that will set your hair tingling. There are some truly beautiful weaves in these premium fabrics, allowing women to come up with something as smart as a man's suit whilst remaining thoroughly feminine.

Superfine suiting makes up wonderfully, doesn't hold on to creases and wears really well. It is perfect for smart summer wear as it breathes naturally, keeping you cool or warmed up as needed.

WOOL CREPE

This is a broken twill, made with highly twisted yarns and it can be truly sophisticated and especially elegant. When made up, it drapes beautifully and has a distinct texture that doesn't crease. Beware when buying crepes that there is no scrimping; a poor quality cloth will announce itself all too clearly. If you really want to go to town, a double knit crepe will have extra weight and give a deep, luxurious drape to create an instant, lasting impression.

GABARDINE

Gabardine, invented by Burberry in the nineteenth century, is tightly woven from worsted yarn. The straight, parallel fibres and ribbed diagonal twill weave make for a tough, stiff cloth, which was the

Wool has been spun and woven by the tribes of northern Europe for at least 12,000 years and has been a staple of British manufacture for over a century. The core principles of spinning and weaving remain unchanged since our ancient ancestors first twisted raw wool into yarn and wove it on a crude loom. It is the historic reason that our countryside is dotted with sheep.

bane of many a childhood in raincoat form. It is magnificent for coats and heavy trousers, can be used for toughened hole-proof pockets and, when waterproofed, will keep the rain out all day long.

FELTED WOOL

Simply put, felted wool is matted. This often happens on untended sheep and to the backs of babies' heads; the fibres become tangled up and inseparable as a result of moisture, heat and pressure. Melton, for example, is a traditional felted wool that has long been used for military uniforms; it is cheap, hardy and very satisfying to work with. These cloths do not fray when cut and their initial stiffness makes for a crisp, bold silhouette. They are especially suited to structured garments.

The British fabric stash is full of lengths of best quality wool from coarse Harris tweeds to the finest suiting and has a reputation for being the best available.

COTTONS

All cotton cloths have their origins overseas in warmer climes, as the cultivated shrubs that give up the fibres of the seed pod for commercial textiles do not fare well in the North European climate. Whilst India, Pakistan and the USA have always excelled at harvesting the long tall plants, the spinning and weaving into useful cloth has traditionally been part of great British industry; 250 years ago, cotton textiles were our greatest export and Manchester was known colloquially as Cottonopolis. Nowadays, manufacture is global and provides us with a startling array of colours, weights, finishes and quality.

CHOOSING AND USING

Cotton is fantastic to work with. It is strong and even, easy to handle and sew, drapes well and can have a neat, crisp finish. It is soft and comfortable, wears in nicely and is reluctant to catch fire, making it ideal both for garments and soft furnishings.

Many cottons on the roll, especially at the cheaper end, will be sized or coated during manufacture and may not be pre-shrunk. Bear this in mind when buying less expensive cottons as inevitably the fabric you end up wearing will be different to the one you fell in love with at the shop. Washing before use will take out any residual chemicals, soften the cloth up and leave you certain that the shrinking is done with.

Although higher quality fine cottons will cost

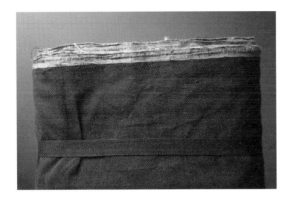

you more, it will pay you to buy the best you can and the end results will reward you handsomely. If you feel certain the cloth is pre-shrunk and colourfast, you may be lucky enough to dispense with the extra ironing a wash requires and get straight to work with your tailor's shears.

Cotton works well for anything and everything, from a crisp formal shirt, through workwear, to a bold and colourful shift dress. It breathes well and can be machine washed. From muslin to denim, brushed to cross-weave, there is a cotton cloth for every project. It comes in every colour and a raft of amazing prints, although you may need to buy a little extra for pattern matching. It is the ideal fabric for beginners to hone their skills.

We have our distinct favourites from the vast array of cottons out there.

CALICO

A cheap unfinished cotton (pictured right) with a low thread count and as part of its simple charm, might contain unseparated husk parts in the weave. It comes in a variety of weights and inevitably will need to be pre-shrunk by washing before setting to work. Calico originally came from Calicut, India and has been a popular choice with makers for several centuries. We use it to create toiles – sample garments to check our construction, shape and flow.

DENIM

Originally a heavyweight twill cotton, denim takes its name from Nimes in the South of France and has been with us for over 200 years. We know it as a tough cloth, ideal for jeans and workwear, with an ever improving appearance as time and history leave their marks. The density and thickness of denim is traditionally measured in ounces per square yard with standard jeans weighing in at around 12oz – the same as we put to use for our apron project.

We prefer a classic twill weave and will always wash first despite some modern denims being advertised as pre-shrunk. Better safe than sorry. Denim sews very well though you will need to use a designated jeans needle especially when stitching several layers together.

OILSKIN

If our middle name was not 'drab', it would be 'oilskin'. It is an iconic British cloth which looks great, is sturdy and easy to work with and topstitches perfectly. Also known as oiled or waxed cotton

canvas, it has a unique handle and will distress beautifully with age. The 12oz cloth we use has a dense weave and is thoroughly weatherproof. Before its industrial treatment, the base cloth is very similar to the tote bag's duck canvas. Working with oilskin has its own demands:

- Marking with tailor's chalk or a pencil will have little impact as your lines will simply disappear, so mark your cloth with the points of small sewing scissors.

- It can be pressed (with caution – the oil can foul your iron) but it is best to open all seams and flatten with tailor's shears. Open one seam up, then flip over and repeat for the other side, making sure you go right to the end.

- Ordinarily oilskin cannot be washed but responds well to a gentle damp sponging. It can also be re-waxed with proprietary products as needed. Dry oilskin sidesteps this with a synthetic wax coat, which allows for washing. We use a lighter (9oz) cloth for lining bags and some dressmaking as it will age and mark the same way as traditional oilskin.

LINEN

Much of what is loosely referred to as linen is, in fact, not. Linen has come to be used as a term for anything with a similar weave, even when made of cotton or hemp, and bed linen is nearly always made of cotton. True linen is made from the fibres of the flax plant, which is easy to grow and does not require pesticides. It is ethically sound in the same way as organic cotton is, and it comes in all kinds of weights and finishes.

CHOOSING AND USING

Linen is probably the earliest form of cloth and was used as currency by the ancient Egyptians when they weren't wrapping mummies in it. Irish linen, though no longer grown on the Emerald Isle, is world renowned for quality and comes at a premium price.

All linen is notoriously hard to iron and so we are grateful to live in an age where the crumpled look is de rigueur. A good pressing on linen can make the finished garment look great, but you should take great care when cutting out linen fabric, and you will find that extra pattern weights and pins are needed.

In return for great durability, strength and tautness, linen demands you enjoy and appreciate the slubs and irregularities in the threads and weave – sometimes a challenge to the tidy mind. Look for something different, nothing too flat; celebrate the manufacturing nuances of natural linen and let the crumpled, slept-in look be part of the style. It is ideally suited for loose unstructured garments.

SILK

Silk is the strongest natural fabric there is, smooth and luxurious, effortlessly tasteful, yet not without its weaknesses. It is highly sensitive to sunlight, prone to rot and does not take kindly to water stains; it is not known for its durability and it will wrinkle. To its credit, it makes up for its shortcomings with pure style, ultimate comfort, warmth, breathability and handle. Cheap silks will look cheap and in use are inferior to good cotton, so stay well away.

CHOOSING AND USING

Silk is full of surprises. First developed around 6,000 years ago by the ancient Chinese and reserved for domestic royalty, it came to lend its name to the famous Silk Road, an historic early trade route spreading across China, India, Persia, Europe and Africa. The precious material and the trade it led to is cited as instrumental in the founding of modern civilisations. Clearly, it is very important stuff.

The thread is created by nature as a fibre found in the cocoons of moth caterpillars we call silkworms – not all moths are the seamstress's enemy then! The inherent structure of silk fibre is triangular, causing the final textile to shimmer as it refracts the light like prisms. For mass production, the larvae are cultivated and bred to consistently produce a white, mineral-free thread that can be unravelled in one continuous length of considerable strength, known as a filament.

Silk is delicate and demands respect. Make sure you use the right needle and silk thread for sewing silk-fine silks. Handle gently and use only fine needles and pins.

WILD SILK

Though not as dangerous as it sounds, wild silk makes up only a tiny fraction of silk production and it is harder to bleach or dye than domesticated silk. The qualities of wild silk are influenced by the silkworms' diet and many varieties are valued for the delicacy of their unique natural colours. For example, the Assam Silk – which comes from the same Indian region that grows a nice aromatic cuppa – has a rich golden sheen that is highly prized for the making of exquisite saris. Silkworms that feed on smaller, domestic tree leaves produce

the finer silk, while the coarser silk is produced by silkworms that have fed on oak leaves.

JUST LIKE WOOL

We have found some truly scrumptious coarse silk checks and herringbone that are woven like wool, and from a distance might be mistaken for it. The treat is in the touch and handle of these cloths, which are literally silky smooth with a perfect flowing drape. Thicker fibres combined with a loose weave create silks with an inimitable natural surface sheen and a characteristic dry handle whatever the weight. Raw silks are chunky and have irregular slubs, redolent of the best linen without the stiffness.

ORGANIC ALTERNATIVES

In this, the twenty-first century, there is a greater interest than ever in the environment and the provenance of our resources, from energy and food all the way through to the cloth we put under the needle. It is now possible to get some really fabulous fair-trade and organic fabrics including cottons, linen made from organic flax, and wool produced 100% organically, including eco-powered spinning and hand dying. For those who want to go the extra mile, here are some choices that often get overlooked.

BAMBOO

A lustrous fabric with a microscopically smooth surface that feels like cashmere on the skin, bamboo has beautiful drape. It is warm in the cold and cool in the heat, and is anti-static. Added to these impressive wearable credentials, it is also hard to find fault with its production. It does not require any pesticide treatment when growing (so the cloth is less likely to irritate the skin), it brings wealth to developing communities and it has ten times the yield per acre of cotton. It is more widely available than ever, so have a search online, order some and you will also have an extra talking point at dinner parties.

NETTLE

Making cloth from stinging nettles is not new but is making a comeback in the eco revolution. With a heritage spanning 2,000 years its last surge in popularity was in World War II, when the Allied control of cotton led to some fine German nettle parachutes.

Similar to heavy linen in its handle and stiffness, the new generation of nettle cloth has been produced as jeans and jackets and takes advantage of the stinging nettle's hollow fibres for great insulation. It is often dyed in its own juices to create a characteristic green tone.

For its eco checklist, nettles can and do grow pretty much everywhere there is rain, including the Himalayas, allowing small communities to generate income without industrialisation. Nettles are hardy perennials that do not need pesticides, taking the sting out of your new-found cloth.

HEMP

As a yarn, hemp is extremely versatile, used in everything from rope to T-shirts. It can emulate wool and canvas and is softer, stronger and more durable than cotton. The fibres are porous for added breathability. By all accounts, hemp is something of a wonder plant. Almost every part of hemp has a use beneficial to mankind. It has been cultivated for over 6,000 years and before the widespread cultivation of cotton, it was the crop most put to use for clothing. It is now the pre-eminent alternative to cotton and the easiest to find as cloth in various guises.

RECYCLING IN ACTION

When we were growing up 'recycling' and 'clothes' were two words that had never met. In those poorer times, however, mothers were not afraid to take down the curtains, draw around a supine child and come up with a literally startling outfit. A careful rummage at the local charity shop may uncover some real gems that can be reworked to make something truly original. The added element of chance can be inspirational. But not always.

PRESSING MATTERS

A USER'S GUIDE TO GOOD FLATTENING

A garment that is beautifully sewn but badly pressed[1] will always look home-made.
A good iron is a sensible investment, second only to the sewing machine.

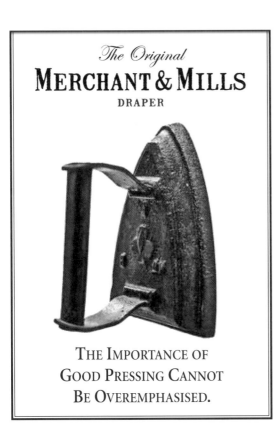

The Original
MERCHANT & MILLS
DRAPER

THE IMPORTANCE OF GOOD PRESSING CANNOT BE OVEREMPHASISED.

- Remove all tacking and pins before pressing.
- Each element of the construction should be pressed beautifully so that all seams sit flat and are pucker free.
- Pressing helps the stitches sink down into the fabric and so give a professional finish.
- Press rather than iron, letting the iron do the work as you lift and put it down rather than moving it around on the fabric.
- Let the steam set after pressing so the fabric cools in position.
- If pressing with a damp cloth, allow the fabric to dry completely before removing it from the board or the garment will lose its finish.
- Never over press. Too much steam will distort your fabric especially on unfinished edges and it will appear overworked.

---

[1] Despite using the terms ironing and pressing interchangeably, a distinction needs to be made between them. Ironing refers to what you do with your line-fresh laundry to make it look smart, whereas pressing is a tailoring skill and fundamental part of the garment-making process.

TOOLS AND EQUIPMENT

In a perfect world, we would all be using a super-heavy industrial iron powered by a steam generator attached to a boiler. Underneath our fabric would sit a bolted down vacuum ironing board to suck out all that steam and leave our garments cool and dry. In our day to day practical reality, we can consider the best of these features when choosing equipment. For clothes making, you will need a steam iron and sturdy ironing board. There are many other interesting tools and devices, which we will introduce once the basics have been covered.

THE IRON (fig. 1)

A small handheld appliance used to remove wrinkles from fabric. It is also known as a clothes iron, flat iron, or best of all, a sad iron. The piece at the bottom is called a sole plate. An iron that will serve well and last many years should tick the following boxes:

☞ An iron should be a decent weight – many high street irons weigh very little. A heavier iron (one over 1.5kg) is more manoeuvrable and enables you to utilise the weight of the iron (instead of your arm muscle) to smooth the cloth.

☞ It should deliver steam evenly in a controlled manner with the capacity to deliver a powerful shot of steam when needed.

☞ Teflon or similar non-stick coatings are preferable and easy to care for. Modern finishes encourage the iron to glide.

☞ A long, heat-resistant flex is most useful. There are few thing more frustrating than pulling the plug from the socket whilst at the far reach of a short cord.

THE IRONING BOARD (fig. 2)

A portable, foldable table with a heat-resistant surface. The seamstress is best served by a hard and sturdy metal ironing board, ideally with holes beneath the cover for steam to escape.

It is essential to have a thick, even cover with no lumps and bumps, and you should set the board up at the correct height to avoid backache. Make yourself a removable cover to reflect your personal style (see project on page 80). Think: If I were an ironing board, what would I look like?

THE PRESSING CLOTH (fig. 3)

Protects your garment from shine and imparts moisture. A damp cloth allows you to press the face of a garment without creating shine. Extra moisture can help achieve perfectly flat seams.

Linen is best as a pressing cloth as it retains moisture without becoming too wet. Cotton works well too, whilst using lightly dampened wool is good for fabrics with pile, helping to prevent crushing the fabric. All pressing cloths should first be softened by washing.

THE TAILOR'S HAM AND SLEEVE ROLL (fig. 4)

Traditional padded shapes made from both cotton and wool and tightly packed with coarse sawdust. The shapes may vary yet the purpose remains similar. Specialist sewing retailers do sell hams but they are so easy to make we want you to do it yourself – see project on page 76.

These contoured pressing aids have one face in cotton for flat fabrics and the other in wool for fabrics with nap (or pile). The curved surfaces allow you to press awkward shapes such as darts, sleeve heads and curved seams. Manoeuvre the curved or tapered area to a matching curve on the ham. The results will be far more successful than pressing on a flat surface.

THE SLEEVE BOARD (fig. 5)

Resembles a small, narrow ironing board and enables perfect sleeve pressing. A proper sleeve board may be considered a luxury in the sewing room, yet it makes light work of an otherwise very tricky job. The better

fig. 1 The Iron

fig. 2 The Ironing Board

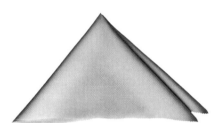

fig. 3 Pressing Cloth

fig. 4 Tailor's Ham and Sleeve Roll

fig. 5 Sleeve Board

fig. 6 Tailor's Clapper and Point Turner

fig. 7 Seam Stick

fig. 8 Needle Board

fig. 9 Fingers

ones have the stand at the far end of the board to press the full length of sleeve and cuffs.

THE TAILOR'S CLAPPER AND POINT TURNER *(fig 6)*

Used to flatten thick facings, collars or buttonholes where a lot of pressing is needed and an iron alone will not do the job. Traditionally made from hard wood, there are two schools of thought on how best to use this traditional device. It can either be used by steaming the fabric, placing the clapper on top and pressing down with all the force you can muster, or by steaming and then whacking the area with the clapper until the seam is cool and quite flat. A clapper may have point turners in the handle, allowing you to press into hard-to-reach places like collar tips and cuffs.

THE SEAM STICK *(fig. 7)*

A wooden stick with a rounded top and flattened bottom edge used for pressing long, flat seams. It has both curved and flat surfaces and can be clad in cloth for a softer press. A 50cm length of smooth banister moulding is ideal.

THE NEEDLE BOARD *(fig. 8)*

A small rectangular board covered on one side with fine wire needles in a hedgehog style. It is used when pressing fabrics with a pile such as velvet or corduroy. The fine wires stop the pile being flattened.

THE FINGERS *(fig. 9)*

For fine and difficult pressing. Some fabrics will not take a heavy iron, such as fragile synthetics, brocades or metallics. Open the seams with your fingers, steam and hold flat, using your hand to press down with force. Remain in position until the fabric is cool (or your hand is cooked).

INSIDE INFORMATION

The operating temperature of a domestic iron stands in the range of 180–220°C. Depending on the cloth, ironing loosens the bonds between the long chain polymer molecules in the fibres of the fabric.

While the molecules are hot, the fibres are straightened by the weight and pressure of the iron. They hold their new shape as they cool. Cotton and some other fabrics require the addition of water to loosen the inter-molecular bonds.

Pressing Techniques

Various pressing techniques are needed for successful results during construction of garments.

PRESSING FLAT SEAMS

All seams should be steamed flat first (Fig 1) before pressing them open (Fig 2). While you do this you can gently pull the seam to press out any contraction. Press dry without steam before pressing the seams open.

fig. 1

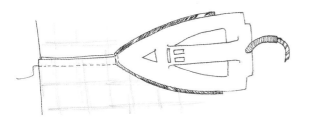

fig. 2

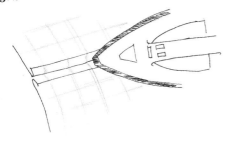

You can use a seam roll or seam stick to prevent the seams edges showing through to the front side of the fabric.

PRESSING DARTS

First, press your dart flat (Fig 3) and then move the dart over and from the other side press flat again (Fig 4). Turn your garment over and press on the right side using a pressing cloth. If necessary, put layers of paper under the dart so that it does not show though. Finally, press to the correct sewing position (usually downwards for a bust dart and to the right on a waist dart). Use a tailor's ham to press on a curve the same shape as the dart.

fig. 3

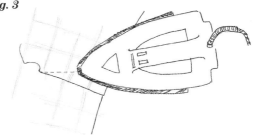

fig. 4

If you have a little bubble left at the dart end, this must go! This can be done by shrinking the bubble out. Take a damp cloth, place over the dart end and hold a fairly hot iron down until the pressing cloth is almost dry. Repeat on the other side using less dampness and less heat.

PRESSING SLEEVE SEAMS

Press open, as a flat seam. It is easier to use a sleeve board or seam roll to prevent crushing the rest of the sleeve. Different patterns will indicate whether a seam is to be pressed open or left closed.

PRESSING ARMHOLES

Armhole seams can be pressed open using the tip of the iron. Use a tailor's ham (p58) for a perfect result.

fig. 5

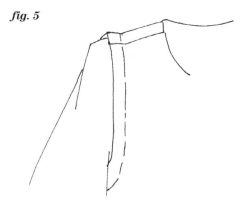

We prefer to give a final press with the seams lying together. Press in the direction of the sleeve (Fig 5) but don't over press.

PRESSING BUTTONHOLES AND POCKETS

These usually need to be pressed from the right side. For best results put a piece of the garment fabric and a pressing cloth beneath the iron to prevent crushing and to stop seams showing through. It is easy to over press, so don't leave the iron down too long.

PRESSING HEMS

Turn up the hem before sewing and press into place. Press only the bottom edge of the hem (Fig 6).

fig. 6

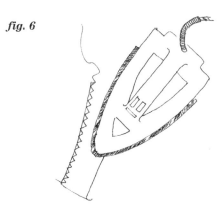

Full skirt hems need to be turned up and the excess can be shrunk away using a damp pressing cloth (see Basic Sewing Techniques, p37).

ROLLING SEAMS

Facings, collars and cuffs may need to have the seams rolled as you press to get right up to the seam edge. To get a crisp edge, first press seams open and then turn the garment right way out and gently roll with your fingers directly under the finished seam. This forces the top edge of the seam up. Press gently at the very edge of the seam as you go to avoid shadowing from the inside seams. This may need to be done on the inside and outside of the garment. Use a pressing cloth if necessary.

THE PRESSING NEEDS OF VARIOUS MATERIALS

Some tips on pressing the basic fabrics you will probably use most in your sewing are included here. If using an unfamiliar fabric always test press on a spare piece, starting with a cool iron temperature.

COTTON

Cotton is not difficult to press and likes a hot iron. Use a damp pressing cloth to get the best results.

WOOL

Never press wool fabric dry: add water to the iron and always use steam heat. Wool is prone to shine when pressed so use a pressing cloth. Shine may be reduced by sponging white vinegar on the surface of a wool garment and rinsing thoroughly. If napped wool fabric is slightly scorched when pressing, rub lightly with an emery board. Use a diluted solution of hydrogen peroxide for a more severe scorch, testing on a hidden area first. Don't over press wool and be especially careful of seam shadow.

SILK

Use a moderately hot iron and avoid using moisture as it may stain the fabric. Thin silks need a light touch. Taffeta is tricky as wax is used in the weaving process, so place tissue between the iron and fabric.

CORDUROY, VELVETS AND DEEP NAP FABRICS

Always press in the direction of the nap. For best results, use a needle board. Lay the fabric pile side down onto the needle board, place a cloth over the wrong side and press gently with a warm iron. Alternatively, stand the iron on its end; grasp either end of the fabric and pressing cloth so the fabric is taut, with the pile on the outside; pass up and down the front of the iron. Do not handle velvet while still warm as it will become finger marked and flattened.

OILSKIN

When pressing oilskin protect your iron with a thick cloth and your board with several layers of fabric. Use a medium heat and press lightly, using the tip of the iron where possible and no steam. If you over press, the oilskin will start to discolour but, as long as you don't overdo it, the colour will come back.

LINEN

Linen presses well with steam but can store creases badly so always press with a damp cloth. Linen can take a hot iron but don't hold the iron in one place too long as it can scorch.

MUM'S THE WORD

Mother's advice was to put a couple of sheets of paper between the seams and the main cloth so that when you press, the seams don't leave tram marks on the other side of the fabric.

If press marks appear on the front of your garment, hold the fabric in the steam of a kettle to remove them.

THE TASKS

THE BEST WAY TO LEARN IS TO DO

The Calico Bag

SIMPLE SHOULDER BAG

This project imparts the fundamentals of good making. It has been designed to teach you to mark, cut out and sew straight, and it is an ideal beginner's project or a good refresher. There is a lot of straight sewing to do, so take your time and try to do it as perfectly as possible. The finished bag is a delight to behold and can be dyed any colour of the rainbow. For the calico label, we have supplied a distinctive Merchant & Mills graphic on our website, or you can choose an image of your own.

MATERIALS & TOOLS YOU WILL NEED

- Natural heavyweight calico 1m × 150cm wide
- Heavy duty cotton webbing tape 1.5m × 50mm wide
- Natural cotton thread
- Light T-shirt transfer paper and bag label graphic transfer
- Dye colour of your choosing (optional)
- Standard machine needle size 80
- Tailor's shears
- Tailor's chalk or pencil and ruler

☞ Wash the calico and the cotton webbing at 30 degrees before use to remove the size and pre-shrink; iron when still damp (note, the fabric will shrink by about 10 per cent).

☞ If you want to dye the bag, it is important to choose natural cotton thread to ensure it dyes to the same colour.

☞ The bag label is available to download from www.merchantandmills.com; print onto transfer paper.

☞ Lay the fabric on the table or floor and mark out all measurements with tailor's chalk or a pencil.

☞ Measure and mark very carefully – the more accurate you are, the better your bag will be.

☞ Before you start the project, practise straight machine stitching on a piece of calico fabric; use a 1.5cm seam allowance throughout.

We have made a label for you to download and print onto iron-on transfer paper. This is available on our website. However if you wish to make your own, go mad with fabric pens or even embroidery.

PRACTISE SEWING STRAIGHT

illus. 1

1. If you look at the sewing machine's foot plate you will see a number of lines; sometimes these will be numbered, sometimes not. These serve as guide lines to ensure your stitching line is always the same distance from the edge of the fabric (Illus 1).

illus. 2

2. To help you to keep the fabric straight, you can place a piece of masking tape along the edge of the guide line you are working to, extending it over the foot plate (Illus 2).

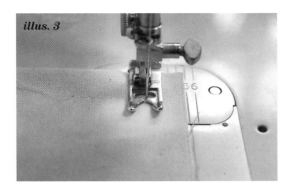

illus. 3

3. We have chosen to sew the bag using the No. 5 guide line to give a standard seam allowance of 1.5cm. If your foot plate does not have numbers, measure this distance from the needle to find the correct guide line (Illus 3).

illus. 4

4. Place your fabric beneath the needle, lower the presser foot and start sewing slowly for about 1cm. Then, using the reverse stitch button or lever, go backwards to the beginning of your stitching. Disengage the reverse stitch button or lever and start sewing forwards again. This will secure your sewing so it won't come undone. As you continue to sew, use your hands to hold the fabric straight, and keep your eyes focused on the guide line rather than the needle (Illus 4).

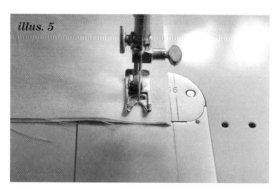

illus. 5

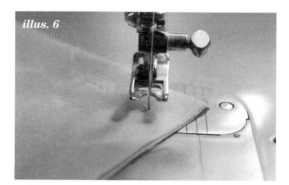

illus. 6

5. When you get to the corner, stop sewing 1.5cm before the end (Illus 5).

6. Lift up the presser foot and turn the fabric 45 degrees to line up with the No. 5 guide line. If you have gone over the guide line, turn the fabric back, put the presser foot down and sew one back stitch, turning the wheel by hand for greater control; alternatively if you are short of the line, sew one more stitch forwards. Lift up the presser foot and turn the fabric again, repeating as necessary until you are perfectly lined up with the guide line (Illus 6).

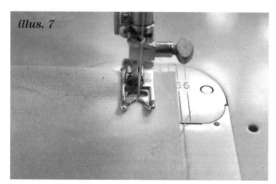

illus. 7

7. Put the presser foot down and start sewing again. Always secure your sewing with reverse stitch at the beginning and end (Illus 7).

MAKING THE CALICO BAG

CUTTING OUT AND PREPARING THE FABRIC

fig. 1

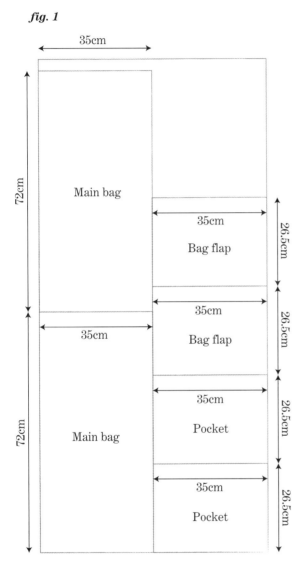

fig. 2

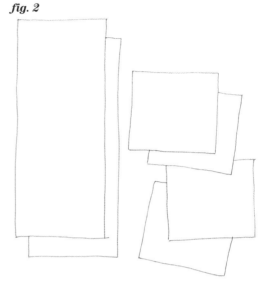

2. You will now have six pieces of fabric (Fig 2): two main bag pieces, two bag flap pieces and two pockets. Each pair will be sewn together to give your bag a hard wearing double layer.

fig. 3

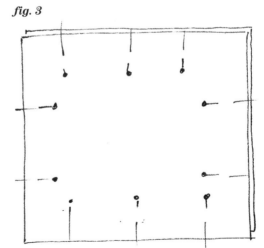

1. Mark out the calico following the measurements given in Fig 1. Cut out the pieces.

3. Before you begin make sure all the pieces are the right size. Pin each pair together. If you insert the pins at a right angle to the edge of the fabric, you will be able to sew over them (Fig 3).

SEWING THE BAG

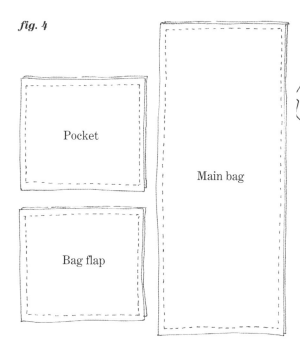

fig. 4

fig. 5

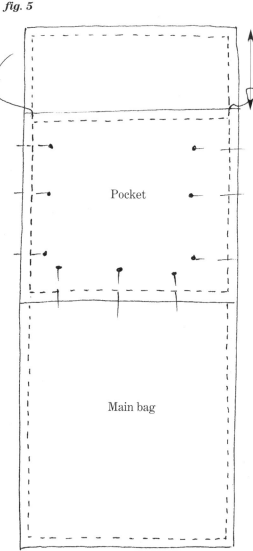

1. Sew all the way around each paired up piece (Fig 4). Take your time and remember to reverse stitch at the beginning and end.

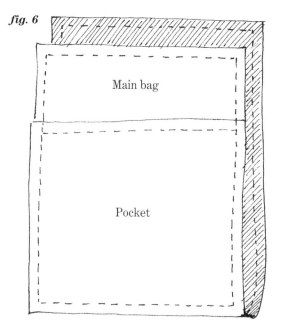

fig. 6

2. Take the main bag and pin the pocket into place 6.5cm down from the top of the bag (Fig 5). Sew on the pocket along the sides and the bottom edge leaving the top edge unstitched.

3. Fold the bag so that the pocket is right on the fold (Fig 6).

4. Pin the sides together and sew down each side (Fig 7). You will be sewing over the top of the pocket sewing, so make sure you sew straight.

fig. 7

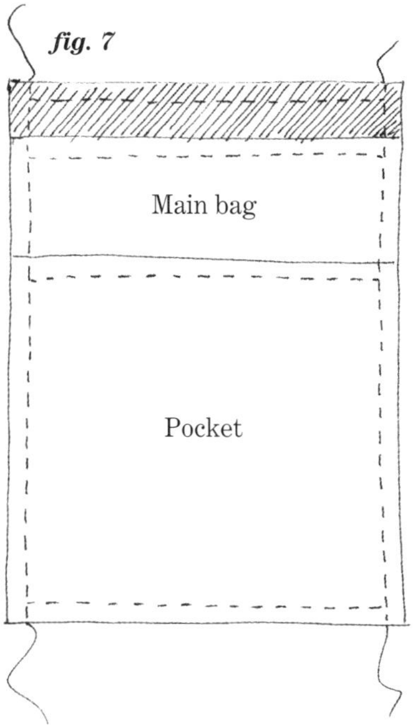

Main bag

Pocket

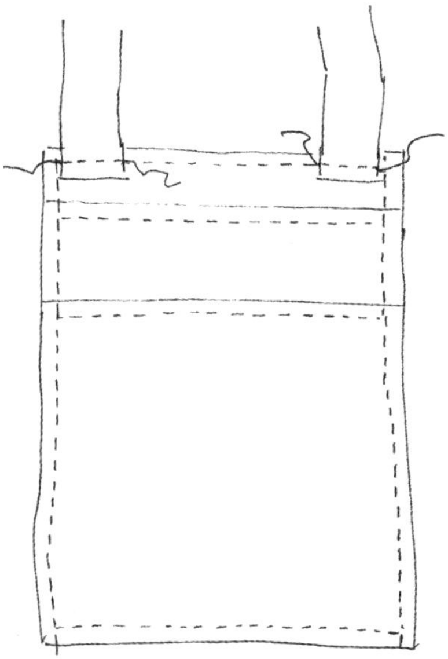

fig. 8

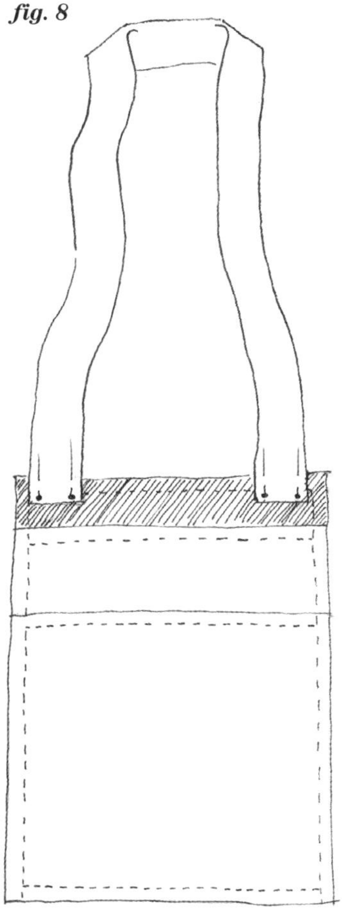

fig. 10

fig. 9

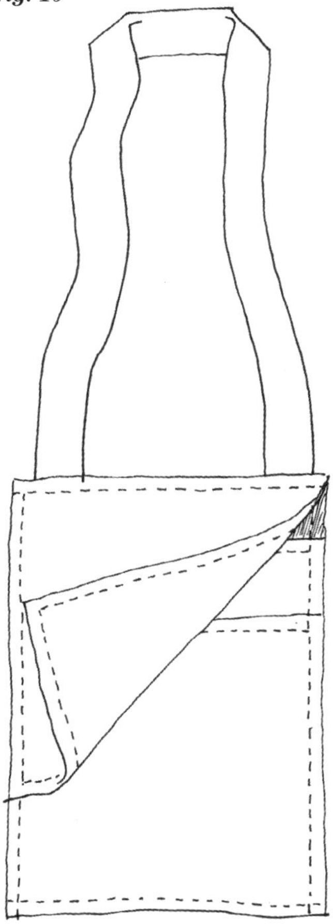

5. Now add the bag handle; pin the cotton webbing tape to the top of the bag just inside the stitching line at each side (Fig 8).

6. Sew the webbing handle into place, sewing along the same stitching line as you have sewn before (Fig 9).

7. Pin and sew the bag flap to the top of the bag, along the same stitch line as before (Fig 10).

DYEING AND FINISHING

fig. 11a

1. If you are going to dye your bag, now is the time to do so – see Dyeing Tips below. When the bag is still damp, press out flat. The edges will be matted and frayed after going through the washing machine (Fig 11a) so trim off the long threads to neaten up the seams (Fig 11b).

fig. 12

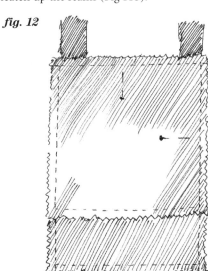

2. Measure across the top of the bag flap and put in a pin to mark the middle. Now measure down the side and once again mark the middle with a pin (Fig 12).

fig. 11b

DYEING TIPS

Calico will dye very easily. There are several dyeing options open to you:

☞ Cold-water dyes are easy to use and widely available.

☞ Natural dyes will give a depth of colour but are a more expensive option.

☞ Machine dyes give great, consistent results (run your machine several times afterwards to get rid of residue dye).

fig. 13

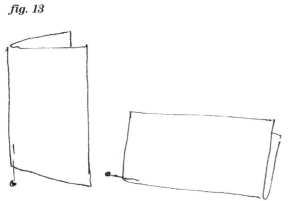

3. Cut a piece of calico 20cm × 16cm and iron on the bag label graphic transfer following the instructions that come with the transfer paper. Fold the bag label in half to find the middle and mark with a pin. Repeat for the other dimension (Fig 13).

fig. 14

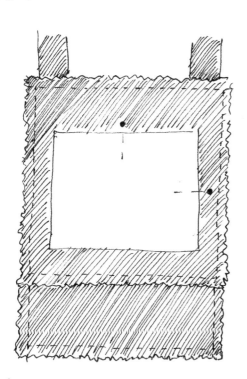

fig. 15

4. Place the label on the bag, matching up the pins so that the label is in the centre of the flap (Fig 14).

5. Pin and sew into place (Fig 15). If using our graphic, sew on top of the border line; if you have used your own artwork, sew at least 1cm from the edge.

THE TAILOR'S HAM
AND SLEEVE ROLL
ESSENTIAL ITEMS FOR GOOD PRESSING PRACTICE

Not to be confused with an Italian ham, the tailor's variety is an essential piece of pressing kit. You may not know it yet, but you need one of these for pressing curved seams and darts, and while you are about it make yourself a sleeve roll, which is handy for both seam and cuff details. Traditionally made with one side in stout cotton and the other in wool, these pressing aids are simple to make for very little money. For more detail on how to use them, see Pressing Matters, p58.

MATERIALS & TOOLS YOU WILL NEED

- Wool fabric 45cm × 40cm
- Stout cotton or heavyweight calico 45cm × 40cm
- Matching sew-all thread
- Standard machine needle size 70 or 80
- Hand sewing thread
- Bag of sawdust
- Wooden spoon for stuffing
- Tailor's shears
- Brown paper and pencil

☞ These projects are ideal for using up your wool and calico fabric scraps.

☞ We prefer not to pre-shrink the calico as the ham and roll will shrink and become tighter with use.

☞ Make patterns from sturdy brown paper following the cutting diagrams (Figs 1 and 2).

☞ Use a 1.5cm seam allowance throughout.

☞ Sawdust can be bought for a few pounds from a pet shop; it makes a right old mess so take precautions.

fig. 1   *fig. 2*

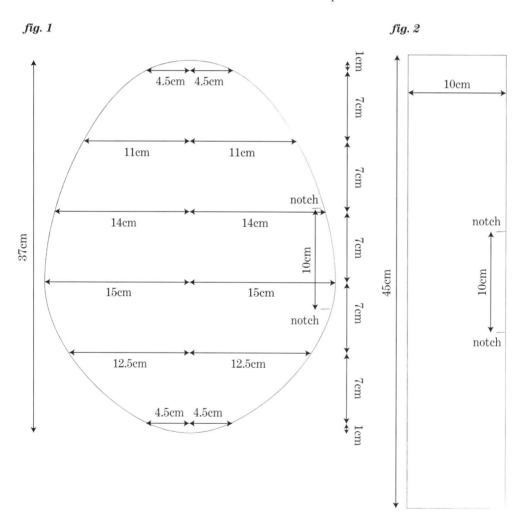

MAKING THE TAILOR'S HAM

CUTTING OUT THE FABRIC

fig. 3

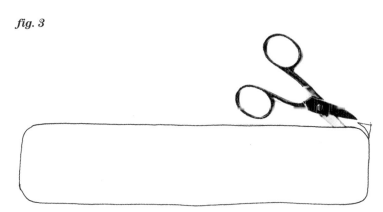

1. Make paper patterns following the measurements given in Figs 1 and 2. Use each pattern piece to mark out one fabric piece from wool and another from cotton or calico. Cut out the fabric pieces, and clip the notches to mark the openings for stuffing. Round off all the corners of the two pieces of fabric for the sleeve roll (Fig 3).

STITCHING AND STUFFING

fig. 4   *fig. 5*

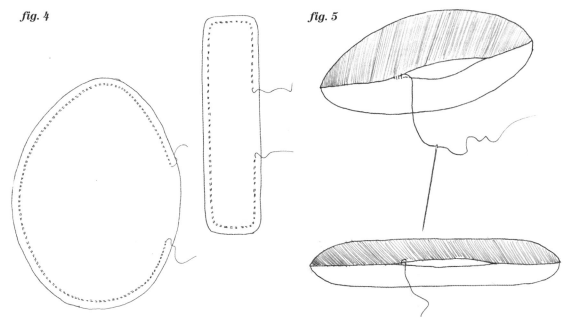

1. Pin together the fabric pieces with right sides facing. Sew together taking a 1.5cm seam allowance and leaving a 10cm opening on one side. Sew two rows of stitching to reinforce the seam.

2. Turn through to the right side and stuff with sawdust. As you stuff, pack the sawdust down with the end of a wooden spoon. When you think you have stuffed enough, stuff some more! The ham should be really solid, verging on dangerous. Hand stitch the opening closed using a small neat stitch (Fig 5).

THE IRONING BOARD COVER

EXPRESS YOURSELF IN THE WORKROOM

Don't underestimate the importance of making your workspace just as you like it; it will encourage you to spend time there. Come to that, don't underestimate the importance of a good, functional ironing board. As you will note from the Pressing Matters chapter, we are champions of the lost art of ironing. A well-padded ironing board cover is essential, and it is quick and cheap to make. An old thick blanket makes good extra padding for the base layer.

MATERIALS & TOOLS YOU WILL NEED

- Natural heavyweight calico 1.25m
- Thick wool or cotton blanket
- Bias binding 5m × 15mm wide
- Bias binding 5m × 30mm wide
- Cotton tape 5m × 13mm wide
- Standard machine needle size 70
- Tailor's shears
- Tailor's chalk or pencil
- Bodkin or safety pin

☞ Choose a heavy strong cotton for the ironing board cover fabric.

☞ If you are using an old blanket for the wadding, make sure it is clean.

☞ Choose bias binding to match the fabrics you are using.

☞ Lay the fabric on the floor and mark out all measurements with tailor's chalk or a pencil.

☞ Mark and measure very carefully – the more accurate you are, the better your cover will fit.

☞ Use a 1.5cm seam allowance throughout.

☞ Always secure your sewing with reverse stitch at the beginning and end.

A match made in heaven: a good steam iron and a bespoke ironing board cover.

MAKING THE IRONING BOARD COVER

CUTTING OUT THE FABRIC

fig. 1

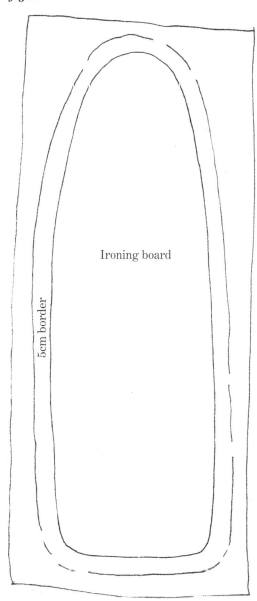

Ironing board

5cm border

Wadding or blanket

fig. 2

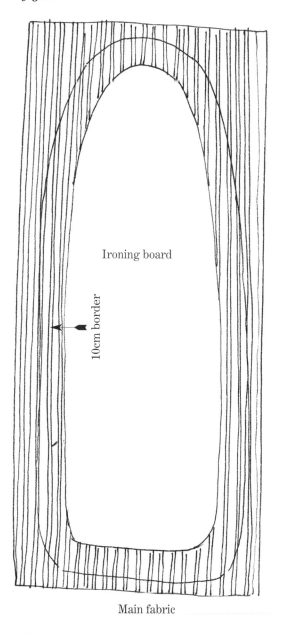

Ironing board

10cm border

Main fabric

1. Lay the ironing board on the blanket and trace around it with tailor's chalk. Add a 5cm border all the way around (Fig 1).

2. Also mark around the ironing board onto the main cover fabric, but this time add a 10cm border (Fig 2).

BINDING THE BASE LAYER

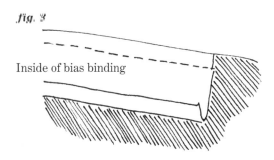

fig. 3

Inside of bias binding

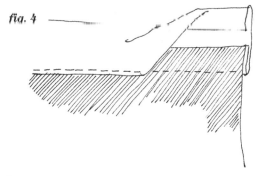

fig. 4

1. Bind the edges of the blanket piece with the 15mm binding. Open the binding on the inside and line up to the edge of the blanket; sew along the fold (Fig 3).

2. Now fold over the binding to the other side; sew along the edge of the binding following your first stitch line as closely as you can (Fig 4).

3. When you get to the end, fold over the end of the binding and lay it on top of your start point before sewing over both layers (Fig 5).

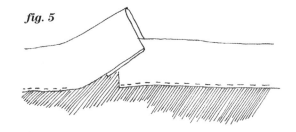

fig. 5

BINDING THE TOP COVER

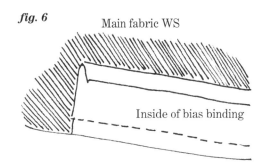

fig. 6

Main fabric WS

Inside of bias binding

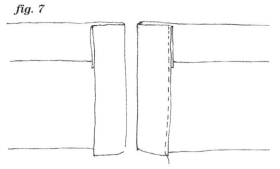

fig. 7

1. When binding the top cover, you will be making a channel for the tape to secure the cover to the ironing board. Sew the 30mm binding to the edge of the wrong side of the fabric, starting at the middle of the short flat edge so that the finished ties will be at the centre (Fig 6).

2. Where the ends of the binding meet, turn over the edges and sew into place (Fig 7).

3. Now fold over the binding to the right side of the fabric and sew on the same line of stitching as you did before (Fig 8a). This creates a channel (Fig 8b).

fig. 8a

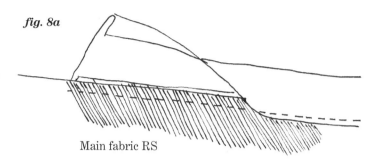

Main fabric RS

fig. 8b

fig. 9

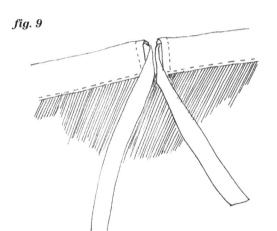

fig. 10

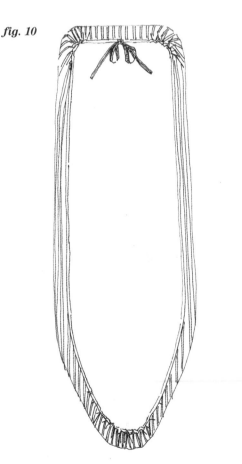

4. Thread the cotton tape through the channel using a bodkin or a safety pin (Fig 9).

DRESSING THE IRONING BOARD

1. Lay the blanket base layer over the ironing board. Place the top cover on top and gather the tape until the cover fits snugly (Fig 10).

The Hussif

EVER READY PORTABLE SEWING KIT

A hussif was once the soldier's best friend, containing all he needed to keep his uniform in tiptop condition. The word derives from housewife and no one disputes the usefulness or allure of that army of women. Our version is made in heavyweight calico and can be neatly rolled up and secured with ties. It will safely hold two boxes of pins, a tape measure, a seam ripper, small scissors, a packet of needles and two reels of thread. This simple project also has a useful ticking needle cushion.

MATERIALS & TOOLS YOU WILL NEED

- Heavyweight calico 0.5m
- Cotton wadding 16cm × 7cm
- Cotton webbing tape 1m × 25mm wide
- Matching 'sew-all' thread
- Light T-shirt transfer paper and graphic transfer (optional)
- Standard machine needle size 80
- Needle and thread for hand sewing
- Tailor's shears and pinking shears
- Yardstick and pencil

☞ Wash the calico at 30 degrees before use to remove the size and pre-shrink; iron when still damp.

☞ Follow the sizing advice provided for our pocket divisions, or if you are brave enough, adapt them to suit your own sewing kit.

☞ Finish the front of the roll with a distinctive graphic transfer, available to download from www.merchantandmills.com; print onto transfer paper.

☞ Use a 1cm seam allowance throughout.

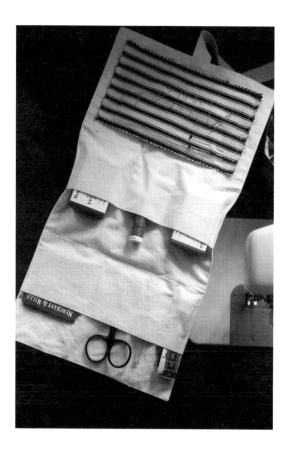

Fill the hussif to your heart's content and roll up ready to take your sewing tools with you, wherever they are needed.

MAKING THE HUSSIF

fig. 1

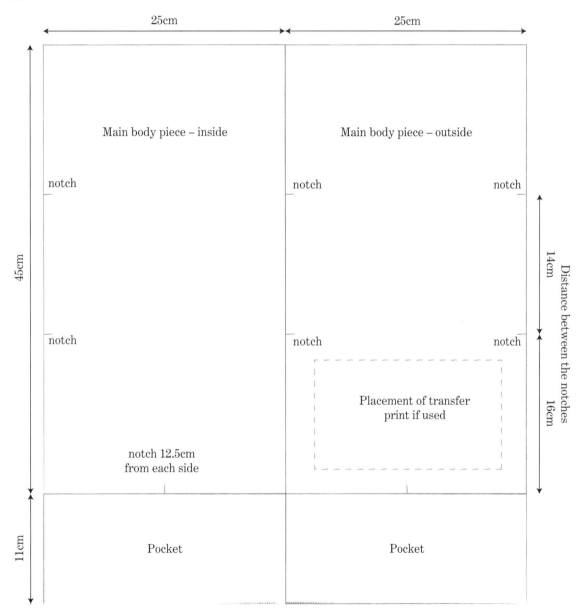

25cm   25cm

Main body piece – inside

Main body piece – outside

notch   notch   notch

45cm

14cm

Distance between the notches

notch   notch   notch

Placement of transfer print if used

16cm

notch 12.5cm from each side

11cm

Pocket   Pocket

CUTTING OUT THE FABRIC

1. Mark out your calico following the measurements given in Fig 1. Cut out the pieces and clip the marked notches.

PREPARING THE POCKETS

fig. 2

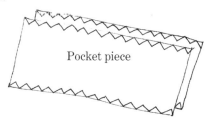

Pocket piece

fig. 3

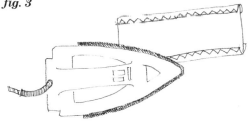

1. Start by zigzagging or overlocking the top and bottom edges of the two pockets (Fig 2).

2. Turn over a 1.5cm seam allowance on both long edges on both pockets and press into place (Fig 3). Use a hot iron and steam if necessary.

fig. 4

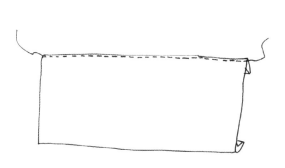

fig. 5

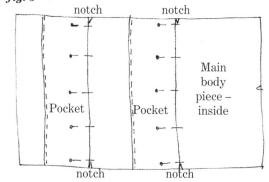

notch   notch

Main body piece – inside

Pocket   Pocket

notch   notch

3. Edge stitch along one long side of each pocket and then press (Fig 4). Take your time with this – see Inside Information, opposite.

4. Take the main body piece of the fabric for the inside of the roll and pin the pockets in place, aligning the bottom of the pockets with the marked notches (Fig 5).

fig. 6

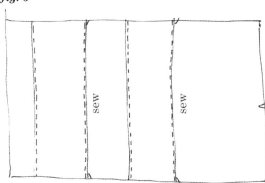

sew   sew

5. Edge stitch the pockets into place along the pinned long edges. Remove the pins and then press the work (Fig 6).

MARKING THE POCKET DIVIDES

fig. 7

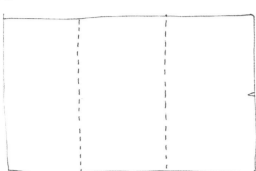

fig. 8a   *fig. 8b*

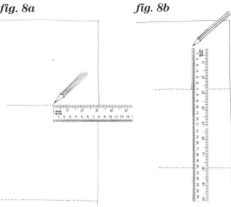

1. Turn the piece over and you will see two lines of stitching on the back (Fig 7). Lay out the tools you wish to put in your roll and measure the divides you need for each one. Remember to allow for a seam allowance of 1cm on each side.

2. Measure up the pocket stitches and mark each of your divides using light pencil marks (Fig 8a). Measure out from these marks to the pocket edges (Fig 8b). See the next step for the measurements we used.

fig. 9

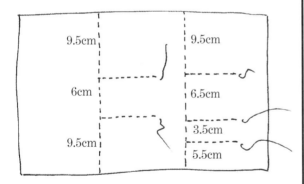

9.5cm   9.5cm

6cm   6.5cm

3.5cm

9.5cm   5.5cm

3. We divided the top pocket into sections 9.5cm, 6.5cm, 3.5cm and 5.5cm (see Fig 9). The bottom pocket was divided into sections 9.5cm, 6cm and 9.5cm. Using your pencil marks as a guide sew along the marked lines. Press the work.

INSIDE INFORMATION

Neat edge stitching or topstitching not only strengthens the edge of the pocket but also gives a professional look.

Take your time, guiding your fabric with both hands and only looking at the edge of the fabric as you sew. Sew as close to the edge as you can, taking care not to go off the edge. If sewing around corners make sure you stitch right up to the edges.

ADDING THE PINCUSHION

fig. 10

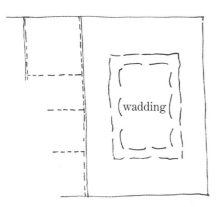

1. Turn the work over to the inside of the roll and use the hand sewing needle to tack the piece of wadding into place 5cm from the bottom edge and centred to the sides (Fig 10).

fig. 11

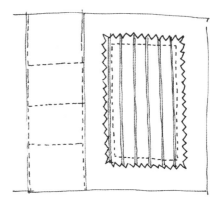

2. Take the piece of ticking fabric and use pinking shears to pink around the edges. Pin and then sew the ticking in place on top of the wadding 3cm from the bottom (Fig 11). Remove the pins.

ADDING THE TIES

fig. 12

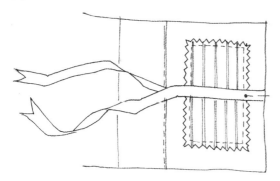

1. Fold the cotton webbing tape in half and pin to the centre notch, with the ties facing inwards (Fig 12).

fig. 13

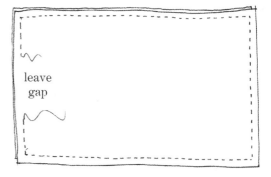

2. If you wish to use the graphic transfer, apply to the outside of the roll now – see Transfer Tip opposite. Take the outside main body piece, place it on top of the pocket/needle cushion piece right sides facing so that the graphic transfer is at the other end of the needle cushion; pin together. Sew all around using a 1cm seam allowance and leaving a gap opposite the pinned ties for turning through (Fig 13). As you sew, the ties will be secured in the seam.

FINISHING THE ROLL

fig. 14

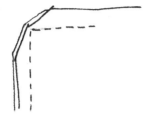

fig. 15a   *fig. 15b*

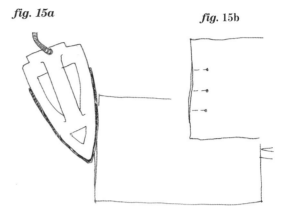

1. Trim all four corners, cutting as close to the stitching as you dare (Fig 14) and turn it out through the gap. Poke out all the corners with a point turner or pair of blunt scissors, using a chewing or stroking action rather than pushing hard.

2. Turn under the seam allowance neatly at the gap, press the opening and pin closed (Fig 15a and 15b). Before you press with an iron it is often easier to roll the seams with your fingers to get a neat edge.

fig. 16

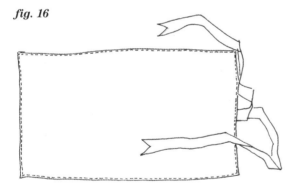

3. Edge stitch all the way around the roll and press to finish (Fig 16).

TRANSFER TIP

If using the graphic transfer follow the instructions that come with the transfer paper.

Position your transfer on the outside of the roll, centred within the bottom 16cm. Don't forget that you will have a seam allowance to take off the bottom and each side, so the size of the area will be 15cm × 23cm.

The Maker's Apron

UTILITARIAN CHIC FOR HARD WORKERS

Our denim apron makes an industrious statement in the kitchen, the garage or your artist's studio. It has some nice touches, such as the traditional crossover cotton tape tie arrangement instead of the more usual loop neckband and waist ties. We especially like the reinforced leather corner pieces which will only improve with wear. The bib and side seams are turned over and stitched to the front of the apron, but we have made the divided pocket the right way around and hemmed in the standard way.

MATERIALS & TOOLS YOU WILL NEED

- Heavyweight 12oz denim
  1.5m × 140cm–150cm wide
- Leather 25cm × 15cm
- Strong natural cotton webbing tape
  3m × 25mm wide
- Denim thread
- Jeans machine needle size 100
- Leather needle
- Four 11mm zinc eyelets and eyelet-fitting tool
- Tailor's shears and small pair of sharp scissors
- Tailor's chalk and yardstick

☞ Using heavyweight denim with a slight stretch helps with the folded edges.

☞ We used a 3mm thick soft pigskin for the two small leather corners at the side of the apron; pinning leather is difficult and can leave a hole, so use double-sided tape to hold the pieces in place.

☞ Carry out a test eyelet on a scrap of denim to master the technique: make a star-shaped hole rather than a circle to leave plenty of fabric for the eyelet to get a purchase on, so making it more secure.

☞ Use a 1.5cm seam allowance throughout unless stated otherwise.

SEWING LEATHER

To get the best results, use a leather sewing needle in your machine and a Teflon foot to ease slip. If you don't have a Teflon foot, sprinkle some baby powder over the area to be stitched and the thread.

Adjust your stitch size to the largest possible; as stitching punctures the leather, using a small stitch might cause the leather to rip.

The cotton tape ties are threaded through large zinc eyelets; these have a front and back so get it right!

MAKING THE MAKER'S APRON

CUTTING THE FABRIC PIECES

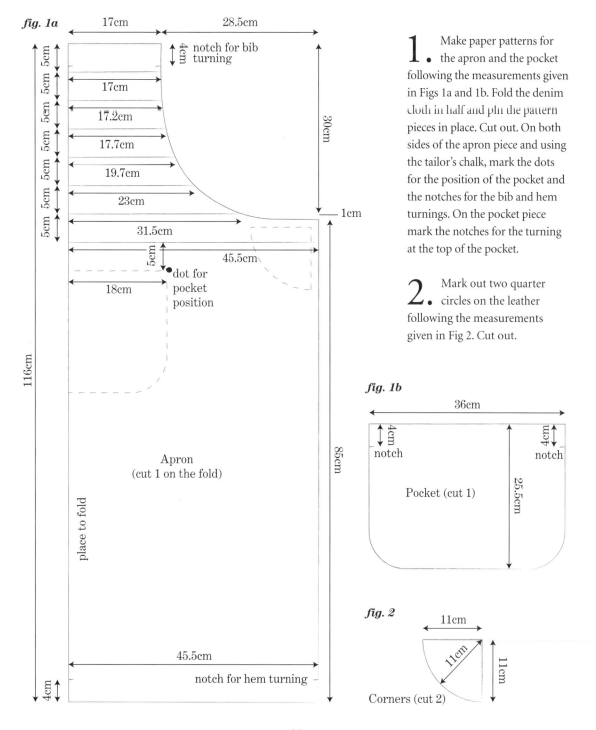

fig. 1a

17cm | 28.5cm

notch for bib turning

4cm

5cm 5cm 5cm 5cm 5cm 5cm 5cm 5cm 5cm 5cm 5cm

17cm

17.2cm

17.7cm

19.7cm

23cm

31.5cm

30cm

1cm

45.5cm

5cm

•dot for pocket position

18cm

116cm

Apron
(cut 1 on the fold)

place to fold

85cm

45.5cm

notch for hem turning

4cm

fig. 1b

36cm

4cm notch

4cm notch

Pocket (cut 1)

25.5cm

fig. 2

11cm

11cm

11cm

Corners (cut 2)

1. Make paper patterns for the apron and the pocket following the measurements given in Figs 1a and 1b. Fold the denim cloth in half and pin the pattern pieces in place. Cut out. On both sides of the apron piece and using the tailor's chalk, mark the dots for the position of the pocket and the notches for the bib and hem turnings. On the pocket piece mark the notches for the turning at the top of the pocket.

2. Mark out two quarter circles on the leather following the measurements given in Fig 2. Cut out.

SEWING THE APRON

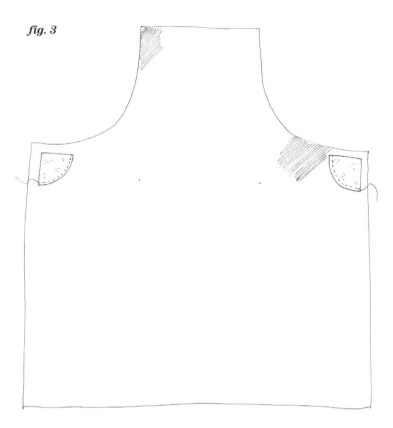

fig. 3

1. Start by zigzagging the edges of the apron using a wide but short stitch; alternatively, overlock. Place the leather pieces 1cm away from the side corners on the right side of the apron as shown in Fig 3.

2. Sew along the curved side of the leather corner pieces 1cm away from the edge (Fig 4a) – see p96 for advice on sewing on leather. Fold over a 1.5cm seam allowance at the sides of the bib onto the right side of the apron – note, this will cover the top of the leather corners (Fig 4a and 4b). Press and edge stitch into place. Sew the seams along the sides of the apron skirt in the same way (Fig 4b and 4c).

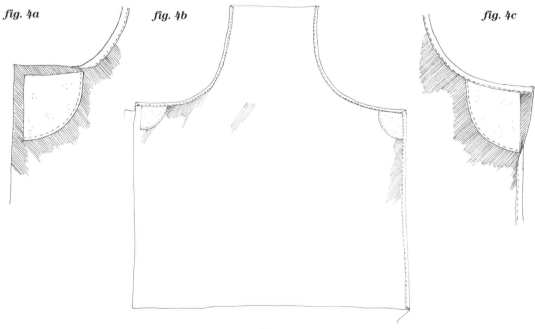

fig. 4a   *fig. 4b*   *fig. 4c*

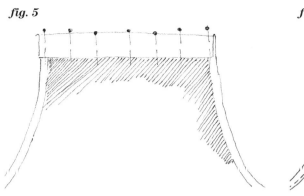

fig. 5

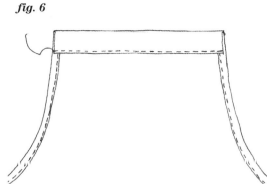

fig. 6

3. Turn over the top edge of the bib to the right side of the apron and pin into place (Fig 5).

4. Press well and edge stitch into place (Fig 6).

ATTACHING THE POCKET

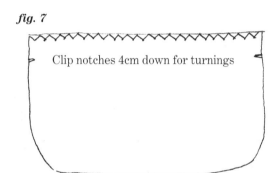

fig. 7

Clip notches 4cm down for turnings

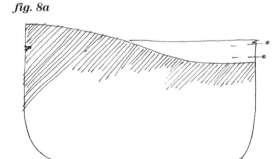

fig. 8a

1. Take the pocket piece and clip the turning notches. Zigzag or overlock along the top edge (Fig 7).

2. With the pocket right side facing you, fold over the turning at the top edge (wrong side facing) and pin into place (Fig 8a). Sew at either side taking a 1.5cm seam allowance (Fig 8b). Trim the corners (Fig 8c). Turn the top turning through to the right side and poke out the corners.

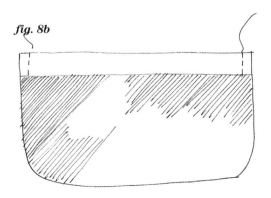

fig. 8b

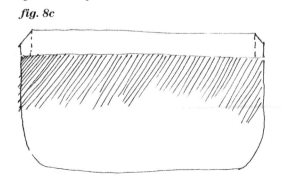

fig. 8c

fig. 9

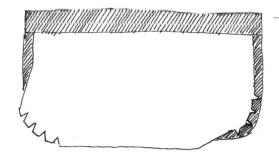

fig. 10

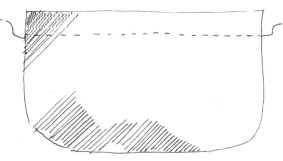

3. Now turn the pocket over to the wrong side. At the bottom curves, snip triangles about 1cm deep; then fold over the 1.5cm seam allowance and press (Fig 9). The snips make a neat curve without bulk; keep pressing until the curves are perfect and the corners really neat.

4. Turn over the pocket to the right side and topstitch along the top turning (Fig 10).

fig. 11

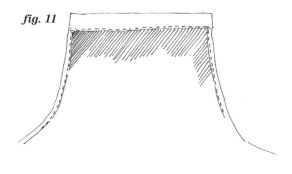

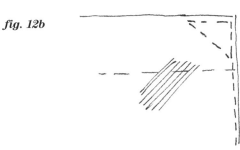

5. Using the marked dots as a guide, pin the pocket on to the front of the apron (Fig 11). Edge stitch into place.

6. Finish the corners with a triangle for extra strength. Make one reverse stitch when stitching the top edge to give a straighter corner (Fig 12a). To make sure that your corners are the same size, count the stitches used along the top edge: 7–8 stitches should be about right if you are using a medium stitch length (Fig 12b).

HEMMING, FINISHING AND ATTACHING THE TIES

fig. 13

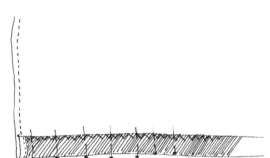

1. Working on the wrong side of the apron, turn the hem up at the notches and pin into place (Fig 13). Sew along the top of the hem.

fig. 14

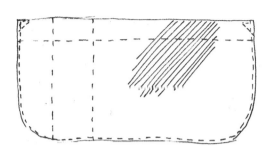

2. Now make the divisions in the pocket. Use a ruler and tailor's chalk to mark to your preference, then stitch carefully along the lines. You can decide on the size of the pocket divisions you want, or have none at all.

fig. 15

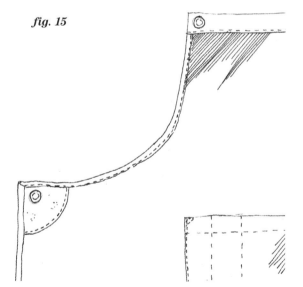

3. Following the manufacturer's instructions, fit an eyelet to each corner of the top of the bib so that the centre for the eyelet hole is approximately 2cm from the top edge and 1.8cm from the side edge. Now fit an eyelet through the leather corners at the top of the apron skirt so that the centre for the eyelet hole is approximately 2.5cm from both the top and side edges (Fig 15).

fig. 16

4. Cut the cotton webbing tape in half. Thread each piece of webbing tape through the bib eyelets, making knots on the right side to secure. Crossover at the back and thread through to the front of the side corners (Fig 16). The ends of the ties can be attractively finished by cutting into a 'V' shape.

THE BOLSTER CUSHION
LINED ROLL PILLOW WITH DRAWSTRING

We have made this bolster to match the white pillow cushion described on p108. You might find that you have to put these beneath your pillows for some luxurious bedtime reading or scatter a couple on the sofa for a lazy Sunday afternoon. It is made from the same vintage linen sheet and tied with cotton tape. The lining is made to the same size as the cushion pad so it is nice and snug. The outer cover can be easily removed for laundering.

MATERIALS & TOOLS YOU WILL NEED

- Feather cushion pad 46cm × 20cm diameter
- Linen fabric 1.5m × 140cm wide
- Cotton tape 1.5m × 13mm wide
- Matching thread
- Standard machine needle size 80
- Hand sewing needle
- Pencil and paper, drawing pin and string
- Tailor's shears
- Bodkin or safety pin

☞ Choose a light- to medium-weight fabric for the bolster cover as thicker fabrics will not gather so well with drawstring.

☞ We have made a paper pattern for cutting the bases for the ends of the lining; alternatively you could use a right-sized plate to mark circles directly onto the fabric.

☞ A bodkin is very useful to pull the drawstring through, but a safety pin works too.

☞ Use a 1.5cm seam allowance unless otherwise stated.

Use a fabric you love and make this simple cushion your very own.

MAKING THE BOLSTER CUSHION

MAKING THE LINING

Do not add in seam allowances: a 1cm seam allowance will be taken from your cut pieces.

fig. 1

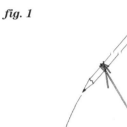

fig. 2

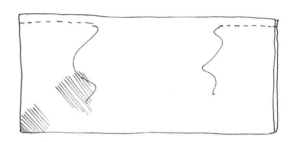

1. From the linen fabric mark and cut out one piece measuring 63cm × 46cm for the main body and two circles for the bases. To make a pattern for the bases, take a piece of string, tie it to a pencil at one end and fix the other end with a drawing pin to a wooden board and place in the middle of your piece of paper . Roll the pencil down the string until it is the length of the radius of the circle you wish to draw, in this case 10cm (Fig 1).

2. Taking a 1cm seam allowance, fold the main body piece in half and sew together along the shorter edge, leaving a 25cm opening in the centre (Fig 2).

fig. 3

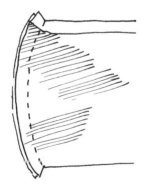

fig. 4

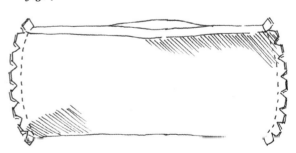

3. Again taking a 1cm seam allowance, pin and sew a circle base to each end of the main body (Fig 3).

4. Notch out all around the base seams to remove the bulk so that when the work is turned through the seam lies neatly (Fig 4). Turn through to the right side, stuff in the cushion pad and slip stitch closed.

MAKING THE COVER

fig. 5

fig. 6

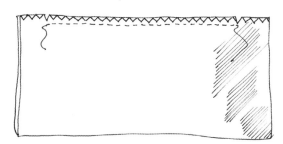

1. Cut a piece of linen measuring 68cm × 63cm. Mark and clip notches 5cm from each corner on the long edges (Fig 5). Zigzag stitch or overlock the long edges.

2. Fold right sides together, and taking a 1.5cm seam allowance sew between the notches (Fig 6). Press the seam open.

fig. 7

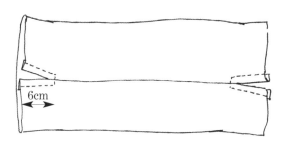

fig. 8

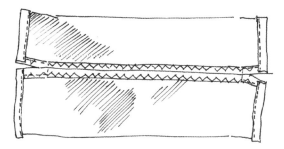

3. Press down the unsewn ends of the seams to form the slits. Turn through to the right side and topstitch 1cm away from the seam and 6cm long (Fig 7).

4. Now working on the wrong side once again, turn the ends over 1cm and stitch (Fig 8).

fig. 9

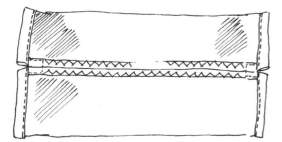

Using a Bodkin

A bodkin looks like an oversized needle with a large eye and a blunt or ballpoint end, which prevents the bodkin from piercing the fabric when threading tape through a casing. A safety pin could also be used, but a bodkin is easier to grasp and the right tool for the job.

5. Now turn the ends over again by 1.5cm and topstitch in place (Fig 9). This completes the drawstring channel. Turn the cover right side out.

fig. 10

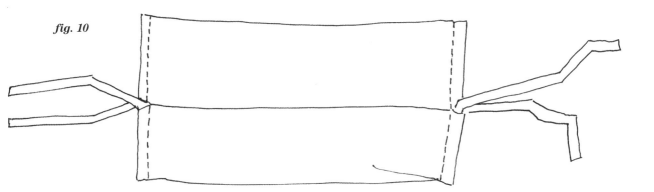

6. Cut the cotton tape in half and using a bodkin or safety pin thread the tapes through the drawstring channels (Fig 10). Slide the lined cushion pad into the completed cover and pull the tapes closed.

THE PILLOW CUSHION

SLIP-ON COVER WITH COTTON TIES

We made these cushions from an old vintage linen sheet which is beautifully soft but once pressed has that crisp and solid look of more quality conscious times. Vintage textiles can be found online and in many specialist shops dotted around the country. Take courage and scissors and do not feel guilty about using something really special – you are putting it to work. Pair with our sumptuous throw and add a bolster cushion for an unsurpassably elegant bedtime. Alternatively, and to let you place these cushions not just in the bedroom, use some muted linen with matching tapes for home comfort in any room.

MATERIALS & TOOLS YOU WILL NEED

- Feather cushion pad 60cm × 40cm
- Linen fabric 0.75m × 120cm wide
- Cotton tape 5m × 13mm wide
- Matching thread
- Standard machine needle size 80
- Ruler and pencil
- Tailor's shears

☞ Make sure your vintage linen fabric is well-laundered before using.

☞ Press linens when still damp.

☞ There are many different weights and widths of cotton tape; choose a fine, limp narrow tape for the cushion project.

☞ Use a 1cm seam allowance.

Simple cotton ties are all you need for the perfect finish. As an alternative to vintage white, we have made the pillows in some fabulous linen in muted colours so they can escape the bedroom and hang out with the throw (see p120) for a spot of luxurious relaxation.

Making the Pillow Cushion

CUTTING AND PREPARING THE FABRIC

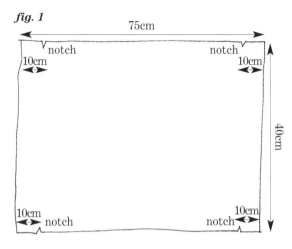

fig. 1

1. Cut two pieces of linen 75cm × 40cm (for a snug fit seam allowances are not added to the width). Mark and clip notches 10cm from each corner on the long edges (Fig 1).

2. Cut the cotton tape into twelve pieces, each measuring 40cm. Take one of the linen pieces and on the inside of one of the short edges, fold over the raw edges by 1cm and place three tape lengths at 10cm intervals; pin (Fig 2, left). Fold the edge over by 1cm so the tapes are lying across your cloth and topstitch in place (Fig 2, right).

3. Flip the tapes back and topstitch along the edge (Fig 3). Now attach the remaining six tapes to the short edges of the second piece of linen.

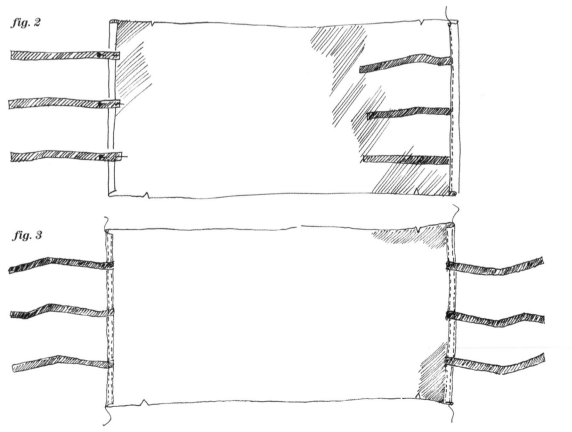

fig. 2

fig. 3

SEWING THE FRONT AND BACK TOGETHER

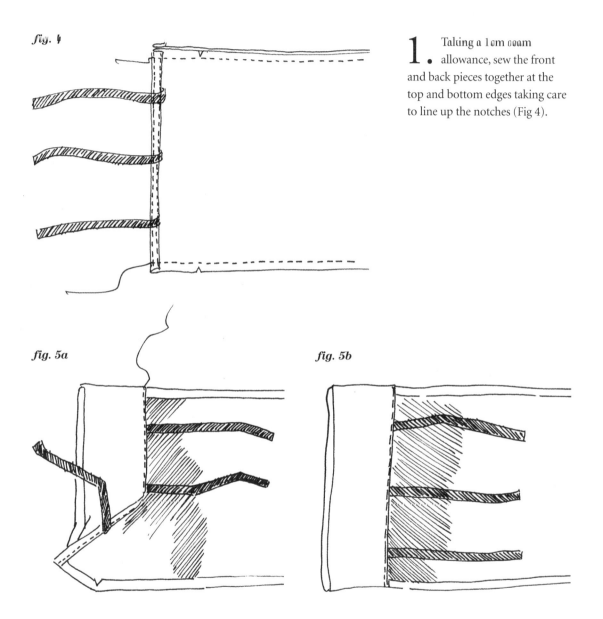

fig. 4

fig. 5a

fig. 5b

1. Taking a 1 cm seam allowance, sew the front and back pieces together at the top and bottom edges taking care to line up the notches (Fig 4).

2. Turn over the short edges to the inside at the notch mark (Fig 5a). Pin and sew together at either end of the back piece only, leaving the ends of the top piece free so that they can be slipped over the pillow pad (Fig 5b). Press well.

fig. 6

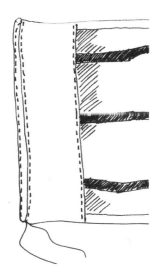

fig. 7

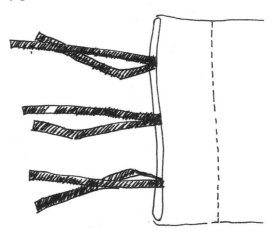

3. If you wish, you can sew a line of edge stitching at the very ends of your pillow cover (Fig 6). This works well on some fabrics but others can end up fluted; make your decision based on how the topstitching looks.

4. Turn the finished cover right side out and stuff the cushion pad into it, slipping the pillow ends over the pad (Fig 7).

fig. 8

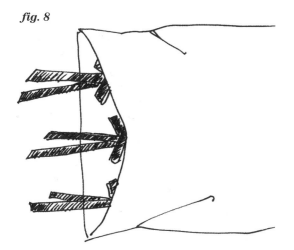

5. Tie each pair of tapes firmly together and make loose bows (Fig 8).

INSIDE INFORMATION

If your pillow is not the same size as ours, do not worry. It is easy to make a cover to fit using the simple cutting guidance below.

Cut the pillow front and back pieces 5cm less than the width of the cushion pad PLUS 20cm: so, for our 60cm × 40cm cushion pad, we cut two pieces measuring 75cm × 40cm.

THE BUTTON CUSHION

SQUARE PILLOW WITH BUTTON DETAIL

Button cushions are easy to make and look really elegant. We have made a pair, one featuring a single large button and the other with four smaller ones. The button detailing is repeated on both sides of the cushions. We have used the same fabric front and back but you could be bold and and go for a rich front fabric and something plainer for the back. The covers are slip stitched to close so will need to be unpicked for washing – most handmade cushions in the interior design trade are made in this way.

MATERIALS & TOOLS YOU WILL NEED

- Feather cushion pad 51cm × 51cm
- Cotton fabric just over 0.5m × 140cm wide
- Metal self-cover buttons: two 4cm buttons for the single button design and eight 2cm buttons for the four-button design
- Matching sew-all thread
- Standard machine needle size 80
- Hand sewing needle
- Upholstery thread and mattress needle
- Tailor's shears
- Ruler and tailor's chalk

☞ The material requirements listed are sufficient for making one cushion; it is your choice as to whether you make the single-button or four-button design.

☞ Choose fabric that is strong enough to take the buttoning, or strengthen your fabric choice with fusible interfacing.

☞ We have used an Indian hand-blocked cotton backed with a medium-weight fusible interfacing.

☞ Take a 1cm seam allowance all around but this is not added to cut out pieces.

We have used the same cloth to cover our cushions and the buttons.

MAKING THE BUTTON CUSHION

MAKING THE COVER

fig. 1

1. Cut two pieces of fabric 51cm × 51cm for the cushion front and back (the fabric is cut to the exact same size as the cushion pad for a nice snug fit). Mark the position of the button(s) with tailor's chalk on the right side of each piece of the fabric. For the single button cushion, fold your fabric into quarters and mark the centre in the middle. For the four button cushion, set the buttons 15cm from the edges. Taking a 1cm seam allowance, sew the front and back pieces together with right sides facing (see Step 2). Leave a 25cm gap on one side for turning through (Fig 1).

fig. 2a

fig. 2b

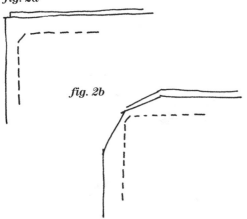

fig. 3

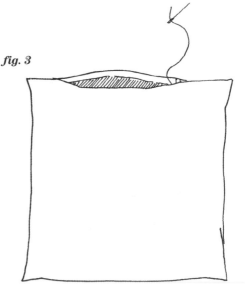

2. For better-looking corners, sew one diagonal stitch across (Fig 2a) rather than a right angle, and trim as shown (Fig 2b).

3. Turn the cover right side out and stuff the cushion pad into it. Slip stitch the opening closed (Fig 3).

ADDING THE BUTTON DETAIL

fig. 4a

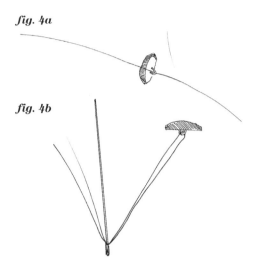

fig. 4b

fig. 5

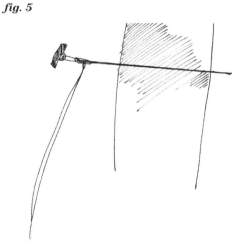

1. Cover your buttons – see Tip on p119. To attach the buttons, take a long piece of upholstery thread and thread it through the button shank (Fig 4a). Double the thread and thread the ends through a doll or mattress needle (Fig 4b).

2. Push the needle through the cushion at the point where the button is to be attached. Push the needle out the other side where the button is to be sewn on the back (Fig 5).

fig. 6

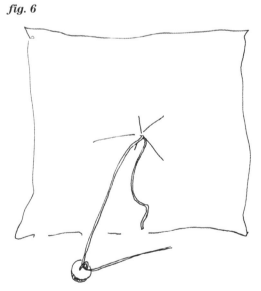

fig. 7

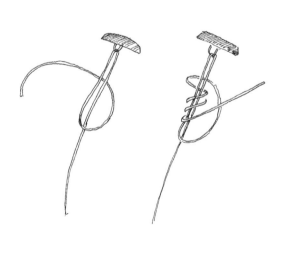

3. Unthread the needle and slip the back button through the thread (Fig 6).

4. Make a slip knot around the back button (Fig 7).

fig. 8

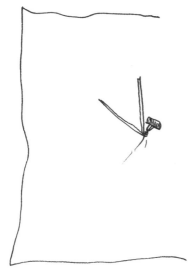

fig. 9

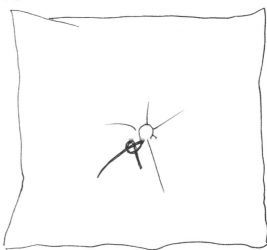

5. Pull the knot tight to the cushion so that both buttons are tight and deep (Fig 8).

6. Use a double knot to tie the knot off right at the shank (Fig 9).

COVERING BUTTONS

Covered buttons are easy to make, just follow the manufacturer's instructions.

If you are covering buttons with a thin fabric, use two layers of fabric or interface with fusible interfacing, so that the metal base doesn't show through.

THE THROW

TAILORED COVER WITH MITRED CORNERS

Transform your sofa or bed with a smart throw. Our bordered throw with mitred corners looks simple yet it requires great accuracy so make sure you cut everything perfectly. The backing fabric is cut larger than the top fabric, then the edges are folded over to make a border. As it is sewn up you must take care to align the borders carefully for an even result all the way around. We have used plain aubergine linen for the backing fabric with linen in a tiny dogtooth check for the top. We love the natural crumpled quality of these fabrics – smart but shabby.

MATERIALS & TOOLS YOU WILL NEED

- Top fabric 120cm square
- Backing fabric 140cm square
- Matching sew-all thread
- Sewing machine needle size 80
- Tailor's shears

☞ Choose fabrics that are fairly stable unless you are an experienced or confident stitcher.

☞ Use a 1.5cm seam allowance.

☞ Remember, accuracy is everything.

With these throws we have chosen complementary, contrasting fabrics.

MAKING THE THROW

CUTTING AND JOINING THE TOP AND BACKING

fig. 1

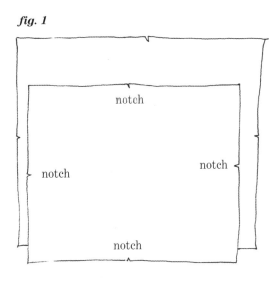

1. Cut the top fabric to your desired size. Cut the backing fabric the same size as the main fabric plus two times the border width and two times the seam allowance. For example, our finished throw measures 127cm × 127cm so the backing fabric was cut to 140cm × 140cm, allowing for a 5cm border. The top fabric starts at 120cm square, and both pieces require a 1.5cm seam allowance. Snip a notch at the middle of each side of both the top and backing fabric (Fig 1).

fig. 2

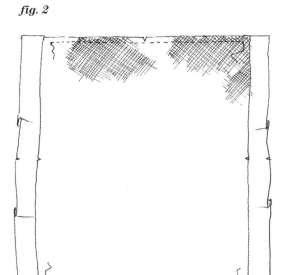

fig. 3

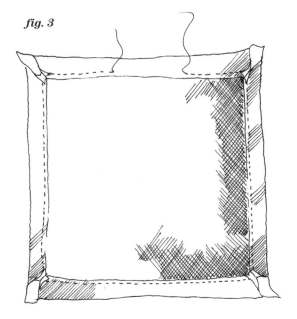

2. Lay the top fabric over the backing fabric so that the notches align on each side. Sew first along two parallel sides, stopping short at each corner to allow for the 1.5cm seam allowance (Fig 2).

3. Repeat with the other two parallel sides but leave an opening of approx 30cm on one side for turning through later (Fig 3).

MITRING THE CORNERS

fig. 4

1. At each corner, fold the fabric down to make a square of the corner (Fig 4). Press to leave crease marks.

fig. 5a

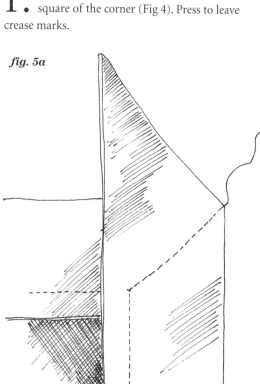

fig. 5b

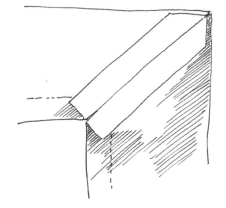

2. Open up the corner square and sew along the crease marks to form the mitre (Fig 5a). Trim the seam down (Fig 5b).

FINISHING THE THROW

fig. 6

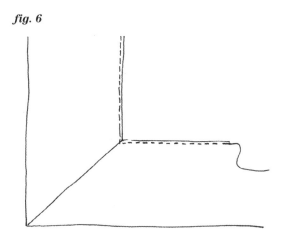

1. Turn the throw right side out through the opening. Measure the border to make sure it is even all the way around and pin to hold in place. Depending on your fabric, you can either edge stitch (Fig 6) or sink stitch along the border to finish.

fig. 7a

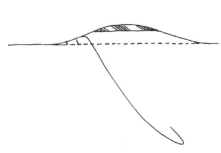

fig. 7b

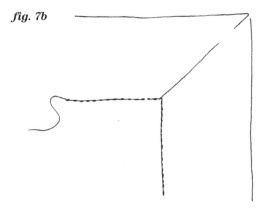

2. If you sink stitch you will first need to slip stitch the opening closed (Fig 7a). Sink stitching goes right into the seam; you are not sewing on either side of the fabric but only into the seam, so the seam is virtually hidden (Fig 7b).

SINK STITCHING

Press the seams to one side and from the right side of the cloth stitch into the seam. The idea is that the stitching will not show but simply sink into the existing seam.

The Document Bag
SMALL OILSKIN POCKET BAG

We have made this useful little bag from oilskin. Sling it around your neck and keep your little essentials safe and close – ideal for the passport, tickets and keys. With this project you will get to make a strap from scratch and fix an eyelet to attach it to. Small as it is, the making of the document bag requires some skill and concentration. On the bright side, oilskin is very easy to sew as it is very stable and topstitches very well.

MATERIALS & TOOLS YOU WILL NEED

- Oilskin 0.25m × 140cm–150cm wide
- Cotton canvas or dry oilskin for lining 0.25m
- Bias binding approx 15cm × 13mm wide
- Matching sew-all thread
- Jeans machine needle size 90
- Hand sewing needle
- Zipper foot
- Metal zip 22cm long
- 11mm zinc eyelet and eyelet-setting tool
- 25mm ring
- 7cm wire hook and swivel
- Tailor's shears

☞ A needle will leave a mark in oilskin: should you need to unpick your stitching, waggle the oilskin between your fingers afterwards to get rid of the needle holes.

☞ We used a vintage metal zip from an old dress. Modern versions are available but don't go too chunky in style.

☞ The best way to open your seams when using oilskin is to use a pair of shears (see p53).

☞ Use a 1.5cm seam allowance unless otherwise stated.

CUTTING THE FABRIC PIECES

fig. 1

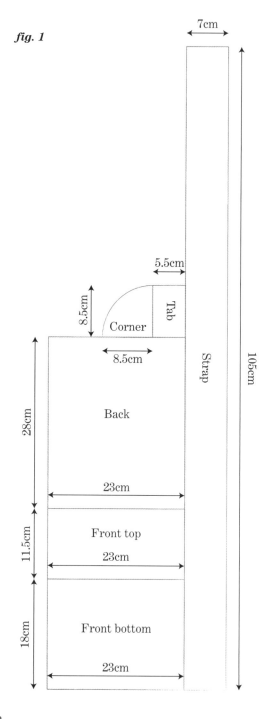

1. Following the measurements given in Fig 1, use the tip of a small pair of scissors to mark the main bag pieces directly onto the oilskin (there is no need to use chalk or a pencil), and cut out. For the bag lining cut a piece of cotton canvas or dry oilskin measuring 28cm x 23cm.

Making the Document Bag

PUTTING IN THE ZIP

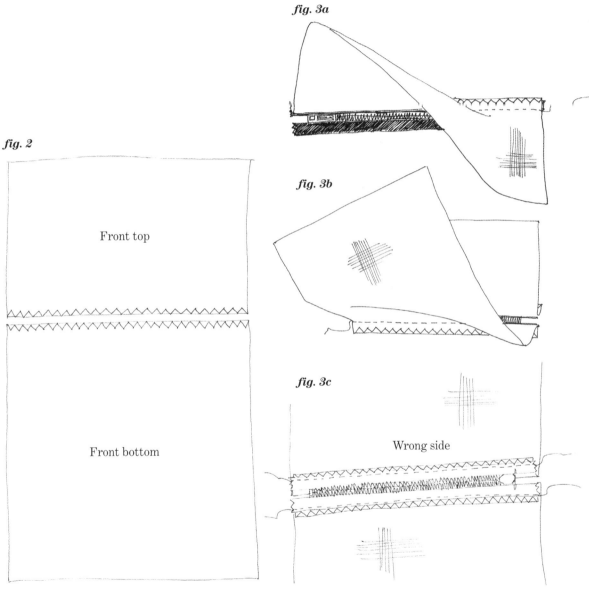

fig. 3a

fig. 2

Front top

Front bottom

fig. 3b

fig. 3c

Wrong side

1. Take the main bag front top and front bottom pieces and zigzag (or overlock) along the edges where the zip will be inserted, as shown in Fig 2.

2. First the zip is stitched to hold it in place (you can tack it before you sew if you prefer). Using the zipper foot, and with right sides facing and edges aligning, sew the zip to the front top (Fig 3a), then to the front bottom (Fig 3b), ensuring that the zip is centred perfectly (Fig 3c).

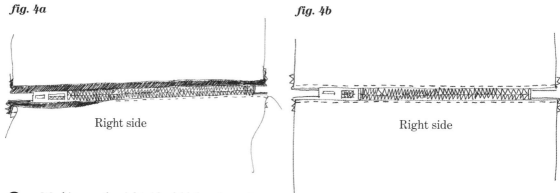

fig. 4a

Right side

fig. 4b

Right side

3. Working on the right side, fold the edges of the fabric over to meet the teeth of the zip, and edge stitch as close as you can to the zip (Fig 4a). Check the zip is even and straight (Fig 4b).

MAKING UP THE BAG

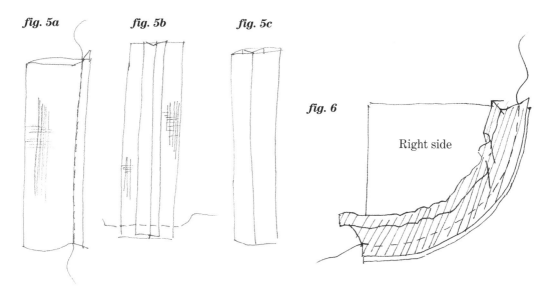

fig. 5a *fig. 5b* *fig. 5c*

fig. 6

Right side

1. Change back to your standard presser foot ready to make the ring tab. Fold the tab piece in half and sew lengthways taking a 1cm seam allowance; trim the seam to 5mm (Fig 5a). Open the seam and move it to the centre; sew along one end taking a small seam allowance (Fig 5b). Turn the tab through to the right side and push out the corners using a loop turner, pencil or knitting needle (Fig 5c).

2. Now make the corner piece. With right sides facing, sew the bias binding along the curved edge of the corner piece, following the fold line of the binding (Fig 6).

fig. 7

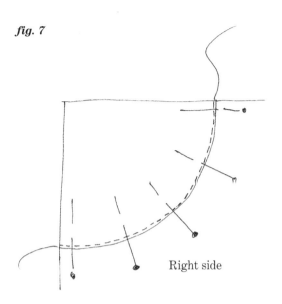

Right side

fig. 8

1.5cm

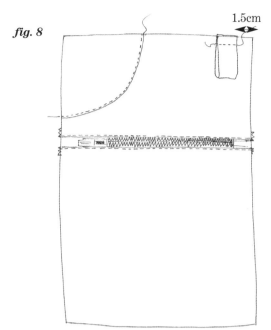

3. Turn the bias binding to the wrong side and roll the edge so that the curve is perfect. Pin the corner piece to the top left corner of the front of the bag (Fig 7) and edge stitch into place.

4. Fold the ring tab in half, and pin to the top right-hand corner of the bag front 1.5cm away from the side, aligning the tab ends with the fabric edge. Sew into place 1cm from the edge (Fig 8).

fig. 9

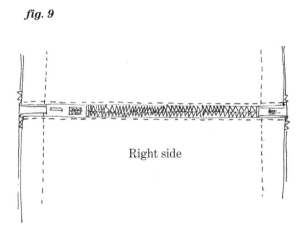

Right side

fig. 10

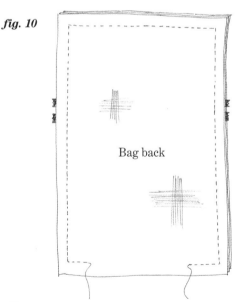

Bag back

5. Place the right side of the lining to the wrong side of the bag front; pin and sew together all the way around. The stitch line should cross the very end of the zip so that there is no gap. Sew carefully; if you hit the metal of the zip you will break the needle (Fig 9).

6. With right sides together, pin and sew the bag back to the lined bag front along the stitching line in step 5, leaving a 15cm gap at the bottom edge (Fig 10).

fig. 11

fig. 12

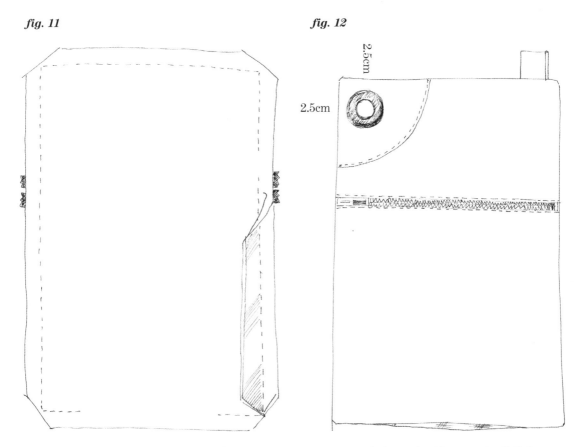

2.5cm

2.5cm

7. With the bag still inside out, trim the corners. Open the seams and force flat using your tailor's shears; press down hard and run the closed blades along the seams until they lie perfectly flat (Fig 11). Repeat through all the layers until the seams are really flat. The better you do this, the better the finish.

8. Turn the bag right side out and roll all the edges until they are really flat. On the top corner piece, mark the position of the eyelet 2.5cm from the side and 2.5cm from the top (Fig 12). Insert the eyelet following the manufacturer's instructions. Slip stitch the opening at the bottom of the bag closed.

MAKING AND ATTACHING THE STRAP

fig. 13

1. Fold the strap piece in half, right sides together and sew lengthways 1cm from the edge, leaving a 50cm gap in the centre (Fig 13). Sew along the ends and trim the corners.

2. Turn through to the right side pulling each end through the gap. It is hard to poke out the corners so try pulling them out from the right side using a pin. Turn in the seam allowances of the gap and lightly press to align them perfectly with the rest of the strap (see Pressing Matters, p63). Roll the edges of the strap until nice and flat. Edge stitch all the way around, stitching the gap closed as you go (Fig 14).

3. Fold one end of the strap over the ring end of the swivel hook and the other end of the strap over the 25mm ring. Pin and topstitch into place (Fig 15). Thread the ring onto the ring tab and clip the hook onto the eyelet.

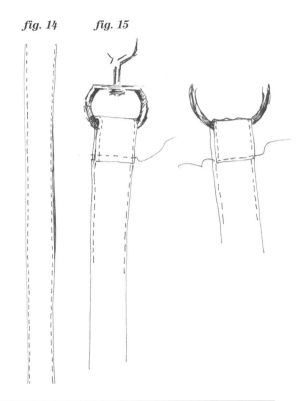

fig. 14   *fig. 15*

THE FLIGHT BAG
VINTAGE INSPIRED OILSKIN SHOULDER BAG

Our flight bag likes to travel. It has outer slip pockets for magazines and the things you like to keep handy whilst the shoulder strap keeps your hands free to rummage for your passport and boarding pass. It is equally happy to travel by bus or bicycle and makes a strong style statement wherever it goes. It is inspired by PVC Pan Am wonders of the seventies and updated to a contemporary take in lovely oilskin.

MATERIALS & TOOLS YOU WILL NEED

- Oilskin 1m × 140cm–150cm wide
- Canvas lining 70cm × 120cm wide
- 4mm thick saddle leather strip 84.5cm × 2.5cm
- Buckram 1m
- Matching sew-all thread
- Jeans machine needle size 90
- Zipper foot
- Closed-end medium-weight metal zip 36cm long
- Two 40mm D rings
- Four 7mm nickel rivets and hammer
- Revolving hole punch
- Tailor's shears and small sharp scissors
- Yardstick

☞ A needle will leave a mark in oilskin; should you need to unpick your stitching, waggle the oilskin between your fingers afterwards to get rid of the needle holes.

☞ Instead of pressing, we suggest you use your dressmaking shears to open the seams. Press down hard and run the closed blades of the scissors along the seams until they lie perfectly flat, but do not do this for the pocket.

☞ Use a 1.5cm seam allowance unless stated otherwise.

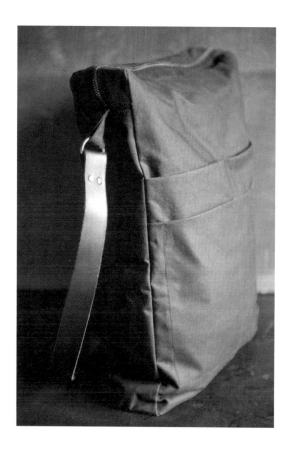

Make a bold style statement wherever you go with the retro inspired flight bag.

MAKING THE FLIGHT BAG

CUTTING THE FABRIC PIECES

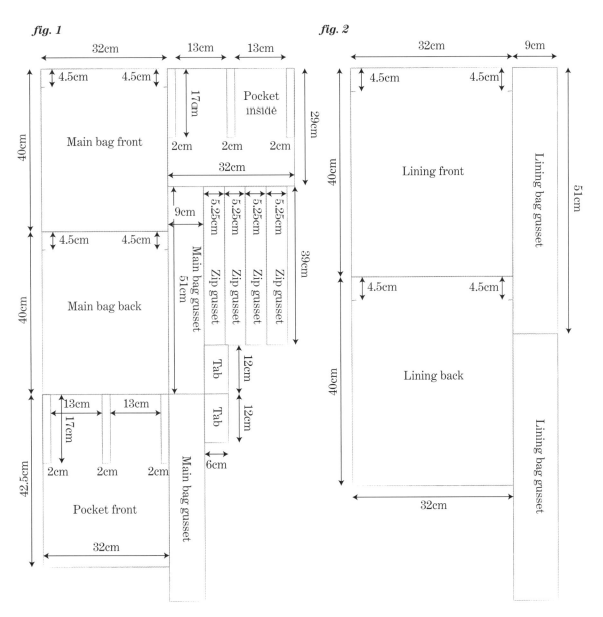

fig. 1

fig. 2

1. Following the measurements given in Fig 1, use the tip of a small pair of scissors to mark the main bag pieces directly onto the oilskin including notch marks (there is no need to use chalk or a pencil); cut out. Clip all notches after cutting out.

2. Mark out the canvas for the lining following the measurements given in Fig 2 and remembering to mark the notches. Cut out the pieces and clip the notches. Also cut two bag gusset pieces from the buckram.

PREPARING THE ZIP SECTION

1. Pin the zip right side up between two of the zip gusset pieces, right sides facing. Taking a 1cm seam allowance and using the zipper foot, sew together, then fold the zip gusset pieces back on themselves (Fig 3a). Repeat to attach the remaining two zip gusset pieces on the other side of the zip (Fig 3b). You will now have a zip sandwich with the zip facing right side up (Fig 3c).

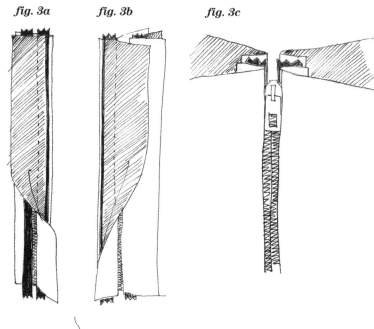

fig. 3a   *fig. 3b*   *fig. 3c*

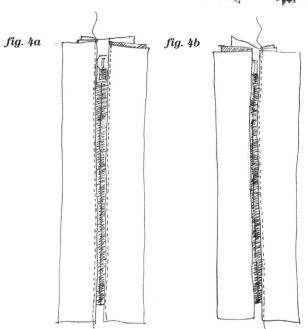

fig. 4a   *fig. 4b*

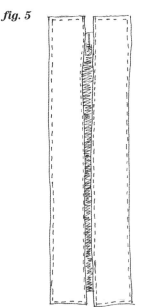

fig. 5

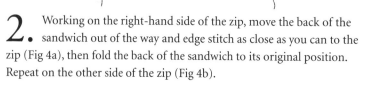

2. Working on the right-hand side of the zip, move the back of the sandwich out of the way and edge stitch as close as you can to the zip (Fig 4a), then fold the back of the sandwich to its original position. Repeat on the other side of the zip (Fig 4b).

3. Now edge stitch all the way around the outer edges to hold the gusset pieces together as shown in Fig 5 (note, this stitch will not show on the final bag).

fig. 6

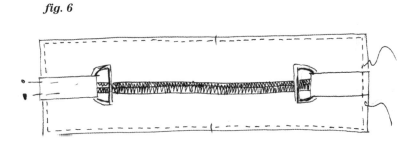

4. Change back to your standard presser foot and make two ring tabs using the tab pieces (see Document Bag, Fig 5, p130). Thread the D rings onto the tabs. Fold the tabs in half with the seam on the inside and pin in the centre at each end of the zip gusset; sew in place (Fig 6).

fig. 7

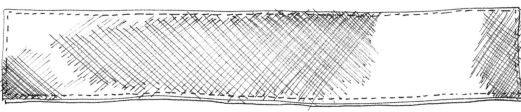

fig. 8

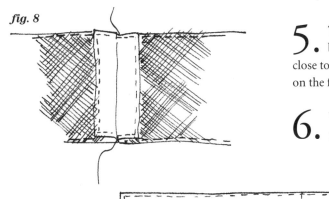

5. Take the main bag gussets, and sew the buckram to the wrong side of each, stitching close to the edge so that the stitch line will not show on the final bag (Fig 7).

6. With the right sides facing, sew the gusset pieces together (Fig 8).

fig. 9

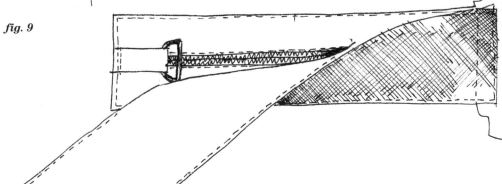

7. Pin and sew the gusset ends to the zip gusset (Fig 9).

MAKING THE POCKET SECTION

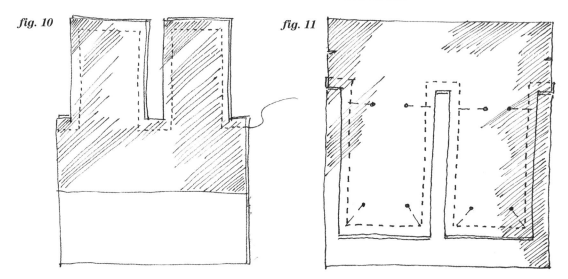

fig. 10

fig. 11

1. Place the two pocket pieces together right sides facing and, taking a 1.5cm seam allowance, sew around the pockets as shown (Fig 10).

2. Fold the pockets down and pin the four corners of each pocket through to the front of the bag (Fig 11). Following the same stitching line that made the pockets, sew through both pieces; this will create the topstitching on the front of the pocket section as seen in Fig 12.

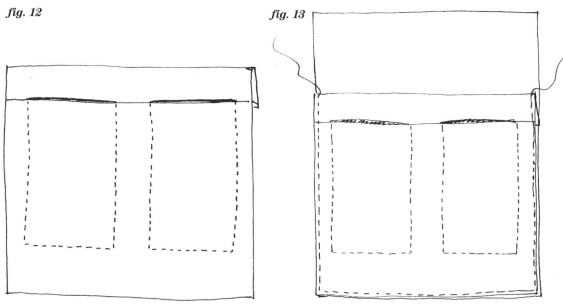

fig. 12

fig. 13

3. Zigzag along the top of the pocket section, then fold over at the notch marks (Fig 12).

4. Pin the completed pocket section to the main bag front, lining up the bottom edges (Fig 13).

ATTACHING THE GUSSET TO THE BACK AND FRONT

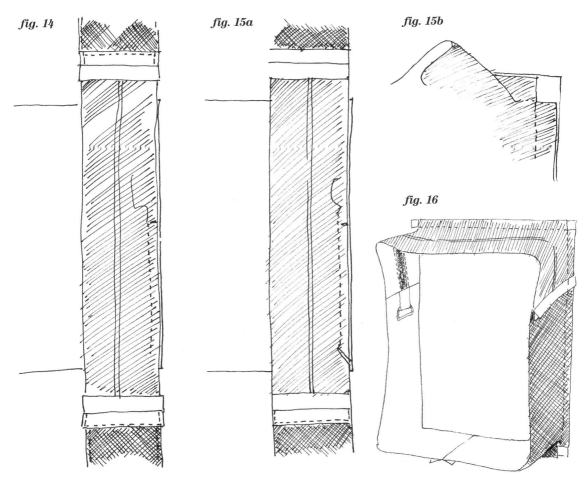

fig. 14

fig. 15a

fig. 15b

fig. 16

1. Fold over the short side of the back of the main bag and make a notch to mark the centre along the top edge. Also mark the centre of the zip gusset section with a notch. With right sides facing and lining up the notches, pin the zip gusset section to the main bag back. Taking a 1.5cm seam allowance, sew from the centre notches outwards, stopping 1.5cm short of the edge of the main bag (Fig 14). Backstitch to reinforce the corner.

2. Lift the presser foot and raise the needle out of the fabric; snip the gusset to the end of the stitching using a sharp pair of scissors (Fig 15a). Put the needle back into the fabric at the same place, turn the bag 45 degrees and carry on sewing; remember to backstitch to reinforce the corner and make sure you move the gusset fabric out of the way before you start sewing (Fig 15b).

3. Continue to stitch the gusset strip to the main bag back, repeating steps 2 and 3 at each corner (Fig 16). Repeat steps 1–3 to attach the main bag front to the gusset strip. Trim the corners.

MAKING THE BAG LINING

1. Sew the lining gusset pieces together (Fig 17a). Fold over the short side of one of the lining pieces and make a notch to mark the centre along the bottom edge. With right sides facing, line up the gusset seam with this notch and sew from the gusset seam to the notch on the long side of the lining piece, which will be 1.5cm short of the end of gusset, first on one side (Fig 17b), then on the other. (For sewing the corners, see step 2, p141.)

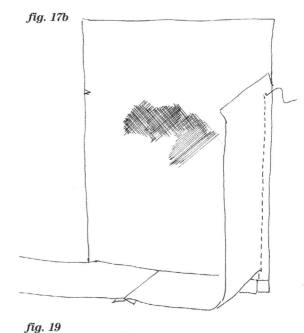

fig. 17b

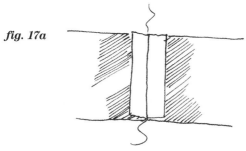

fig. 17a

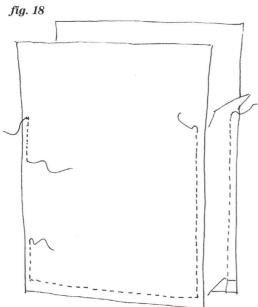

fig. 18

fig. 19

2. Repeat step 1 to attach the second lining piece to the lining gusset, but this time leave a gap of about 20cm in the side seam to turn the bag through (Fig 18).

3. Place the main bag inside the lining. Match up the zip gusset with the lining gusset and taking a 1.5cm seam allowance, sew all the way around (Fig 19). Make sure that the ends of the gussets remain unstitched. Trim the corners. Turn the bag out through the lining and poke the corners out well.

fig. 20a   *fig. 20b*

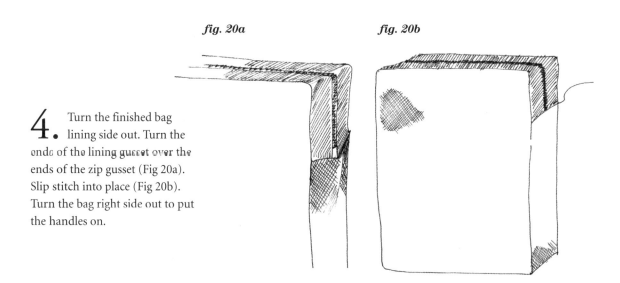

4. Turn the finished bag lining side out. Turn the ends of the lining gusset over the ends of the zip gusset (Fig 20a). Slip stitch into place (Fig 20b). Turn the bag right side out to put the handles on.

MAKING THE BAG STRAP

fig. 21   *fig. 22*

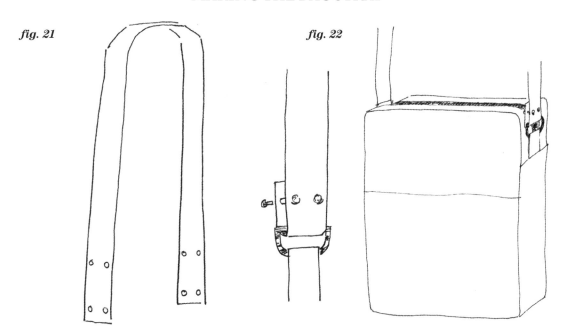

1. Using the revolving hole punch, punch two pairs of holes in each end of the leather strap so that the lower holes are 1.3cm and the upper holes 5cm from the strap end. The distance between each pair of holes is 1.3cm (Fig 21).

2. Fold the strap ends through the D rings on the zip gusset and thread the rivets through the holes; hammer the rivets together to secure the strap, following the manufacturer's instructions (Fig 22).

THE DUFFEL BAG

CLASSIC OUTDOOR BAG IN
TRADITIONAL CLOTHS

We have chosen to make this classic duffel bag from a wool worsted suiting and a matching oilskin. We have lined it with a dry oilskin to make it water resistant. It has an inside pocket, a cord handle, closes with a drawstring and demands to be slung over the shoulder for cycling and long walks. We also make this in all oilskin for a more masculine bag that is waterproof and ideal for the great outdoors. Either version will make for a very desirable gift.

MATERIALS & TOOLS YOU WILL NEED

- Oilskin 0.5m × 150cm wide
- Wool suiting 0.75m × 140cm wide
- Canvas or dry oilskin for lining 0.75m
- Matching sew-all thread
- Cotton sash cord 2.5m
- Jeans machine needle size 90
- Eight 14mm zinc eyelets and eyelet-setting tool
- Nickel hook clip
- Plastic mesh (10-count) A4 size
- Stanley knife or similar for cutting plastic mesh
- Tailor's shears and small sharp scissors
- Tape measure
- Tailor's chalk

☛ Oilskin is very easy to work with; it is very stable and topstitches beautifully.

☛ You can press oilskin as long as you don't leave the iron down for very long; do not use steam; protect your iron and the ironing board.

☛ Cut two paper circle patterns, one with a radius of 14.5cm and one with a radius of 12.5cm, using the method described in the Bolster Cushion (see Fig 1, p105).

☛ Topstitch with extra care as you will have to live with it.

☛ Use a 1.5cm seam allowance unless otherwise stated.

MAKING THE DUFFEL BAG

CUTTING THE FABRIC PIECES

fig. 1

1. First cut out the required pieces from the oilskin, following the measurements given in Fig 1 and using the circle paper pattern with a 14.5cm radius. Use the tip of a small pair of sharp scissors to mark directly onto the oilskin (there is no need to use chalk or a pencil).

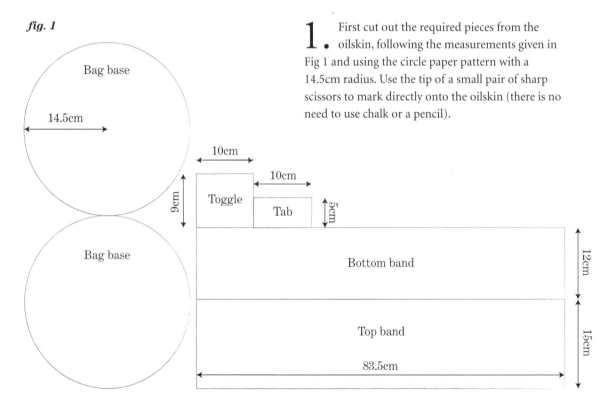

2. Now cut the rest of the fabrics for the duffel bag as listed right:

From the lining fabric
Lining bag: 83.5cm × 55.5cm
Lining base: 14.5cm radius circle
Lining pocket: 24cm × 16cm

From the main fabric
Main bag: 83.5cm × 60cm

From the plastic canvas
Base: 12.5cm radius circle

PREPARING THE FABRIC PIECES FOR ASSEMBLY

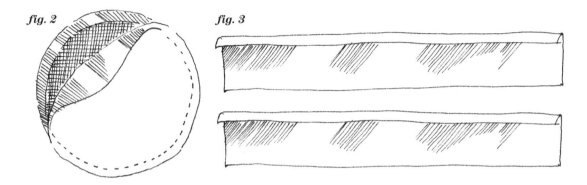

fig. 2

fig. 3

1. Sandwich the plastic mesh between the two oilskin bag bases. Pin and sew together, taking a 1cm seam allowance (Fig 2).

2. Take the top and bottom oilskin bands and turn over a 1.5cm seam allowance along one long edge; press lightly to hold in place (Fig 3).

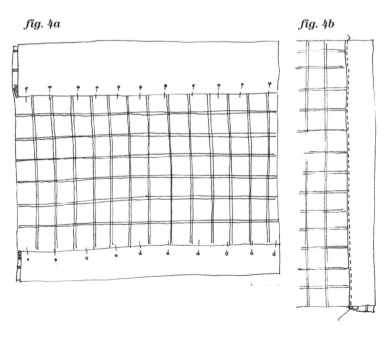

fig. 4a

fig. 4b

3. Lay the oilskin bands right side up (seam allowance underneath) to align the unfolded edges with the long edges of the main bag fabric (also right side up). This creates a double layer at the top and base of the duffel bag (Fig 4a). Edge stitch into place (Fig 4b). Take your time – this topstitch will be seen on the finished bag so make it as perfect as you can.

fig. 5

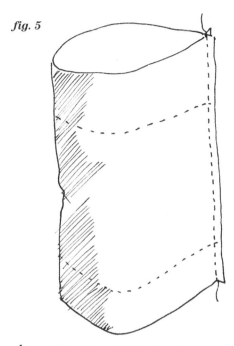

fig. 6

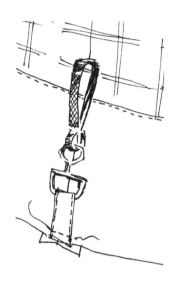

4. Fold the bag in half with right sides facing; pin and sew together, making sure that the top and bottom bands meet perfectly (Fig 5). Press the seam open. Turn the bag right side out.

5. Make a ring tab using the oilskin tag piece (see Document Bag, Fig 5, p130). Thread the swivel hook onto the tab and fold in half with the seam on the inside; pin over the seam on the right side of the bottom edge of the bag and sew in place taking a 1cm seam allowance (Fig 6). Turn the bag inside out again.

fig. 7

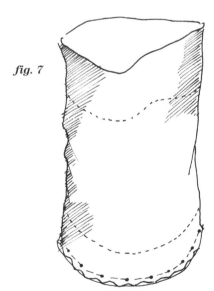

fig. 8

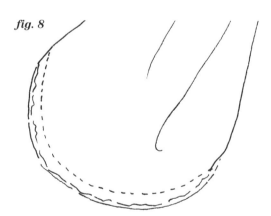

6. Now attach the sandwiched bag base to the bottom edge of the bag, putting the pins in lengthways so that they hold the base in place but you can take them out as you sew (Fig 7).

7. Taking a 1.5cm seam allowance, sew around the base (Fig 8).

MAKING THE INTERNAL POCKET

fig. 9

fig. 10

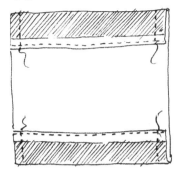

fig. 11

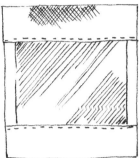

1. Take the pocket piece and turn over the short edges by 1cm; topstitch into place (Fig 9).

2. Turn over the hemmed edges by 2cm as shown (Fig 10); pin and sew down the sides of the turn-over taking a 1cm seam allowance. Trim all four corners.

3. Turn the pocket through to the right side and poke out the corners. Press flat (Fig 11).

fig. 12

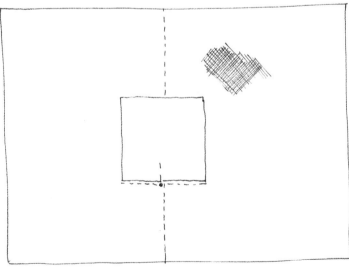

fig. 13

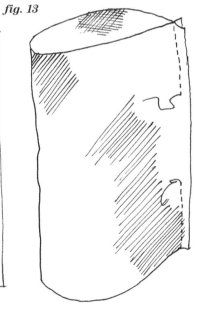

4. Mark the centre of the lining and the pocket. Match up the centres, placing the pocket 17.5cm from the bottom edge (Fig 12). Sew in place (see The Maker's Apron, step 6, p100, for finishing the top corners of the pocket).

5. Fold the lining in half so that the pocket is on the inside and sew the side edge together leaving a 20cm gap in the middle (Fig 13).

ASSEMBLING THE BAG

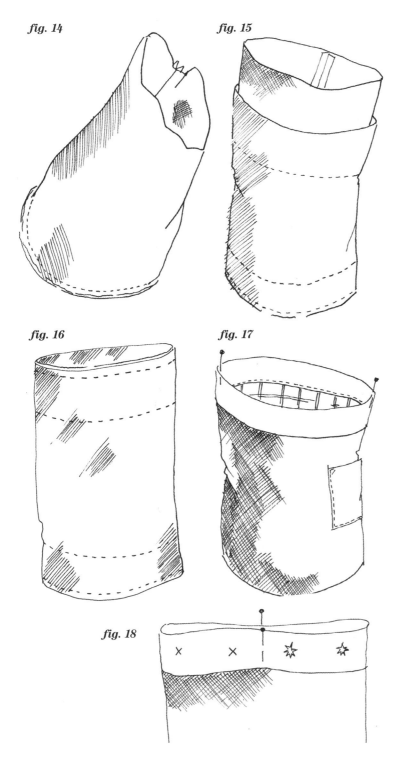

fig. 14

fig. 15

fig. 16

fig. 17

fig. 18

1. Sew the lining to the lining base (Fig 14), and turn the lining right way out.

2. Place the lining inside the main bag so they are right sides together and the side seams align (Fig 15).

3. Sew around the top seams, making sure the side seams are flat and open (Fig 16).

4. Turn the bag through the opening in the lining so that the pocket is on the outside and 6cm of the oilskin is showing at the top of both edges (Fig 17).

5. Now make the placement marks for the eyelet holes, centring these in the top band, 3cm down from the top edge. Working from the middle of the top band, measure and mark 5cm either side of it. Continue around the bag, marking every 10cm. You will have eight marks. Use small sharp scissors to snip small star-shaped holes just big enough to take the eyelets (Fig 18). Follow the manufacturer's instructions to put the eyelets in (do a test first). Slip stitch the opening in the lining seam closed and turn the bag right side out.

MAKING THE TOGGLE AND LACING THE DRAWSTRING CORD

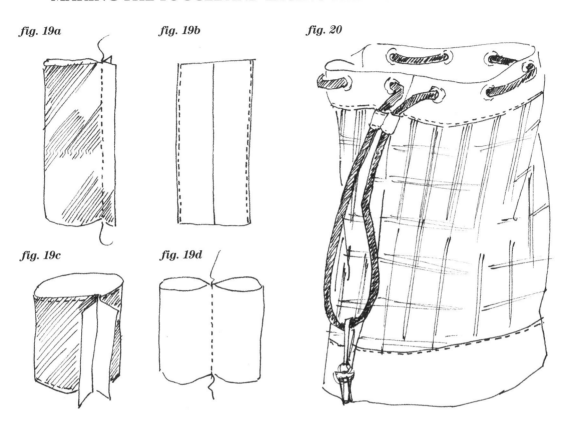

fig. 19a *fig. 19b* *fig. 20*

fig. 19c *fig. 19d*

1. First make the toggle. Fold the oilskin toggle piece in half and sew together lengthways using a 1cm seam allowance (Fig 19a). Turn the right way out. Move the seam to the centre and edge stitch along either side (Fig 19b). Fold over and sew the two short sides together (Fig 19c). Trim the seams down. Turn out the right way with the seam on the inside. Making sure the seam is open and flat, sew down the centre to create two tubes (Fig 19d).

2. Starting at the front of the bag, lace the cord through the eyelet holes. As it emerges out of the centre back seam, feed the cord end through one side of the toggle, through the swivel catch, back up through the other side of the toggle, and back through the remaining eyelet holes. Tie off both ends at the front with a firm knot and trim so that the knots are neat and tidy (Fig 20).

INSIDE INFORMATION

If you are using a sash cord, pull out the centre nylon cords longer than the cotton outside cord and trim down so that the nylon retreats inside the cord and is hidden from view.

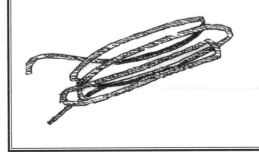

THE TOTE BAG

STRONG AND ROBUST SHOPPER

This industrious bag is designed to be made in a heavyweight luggage fabric. We have used an oiled heavyweight hemp canvas and lined it with a 12oz duck canvas. We like a stiff solid bag so the bag base has been stiffened with a plastic mesh. Our tote has two thick leather bag handles, riveted into place for some serious carrying. For an alternative look, it works well in muted colours and is especially cosmopolitan in a good weighty denim.

MATERIALS & TOOLS YOU WILL NEED

- Heavyweight luggage fabric 0.75m × 140cm wide
- 12oz duck canvas for lining 0.6m × 120cm wide
- Matching sew-all thread
- Jeans machine needle size 90
- Hand sewing needle
- 4mm thick saddle leather strip 1.2m × 3cm
- Eight 11mm nickel-capped rivets and hammer
- Revolving hole punch
- Plastic mesh (10-count) A3 size
- Stanley knife and metal ruler
- Paper scissors
- Small pair of sharp scissors
- Tailor's shears

☞ If you use a slightly lighter fabric it can be stiffened and thickened with a heavyweight fusible interfacing or by using buckram in the gussets (see the Flight Bag, Fig 7, p139).

☞ Cut plastic mesh with strong paper scissors. DO NOT USE YOUR SEWING SCISSORS. Try to keep the cut edge as smooth as possible – tiny plastic corners from the mesh can pierce the canvas.

☞ Use a 1.5cm seam allowance throughout unless otherwise instructed.

☞ Rivets are easy to use and are lined up and snapped together before making the final hammer blow.

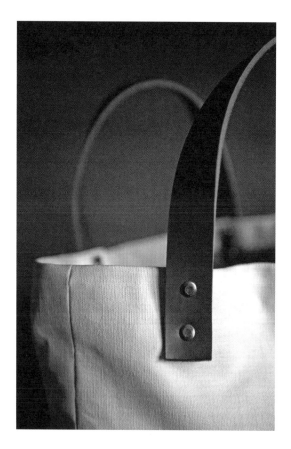

Rivets add a work-wear style look to this project.

MAKING THE TOTE BAG

CUTTING AND PREPARING THE FABRIC

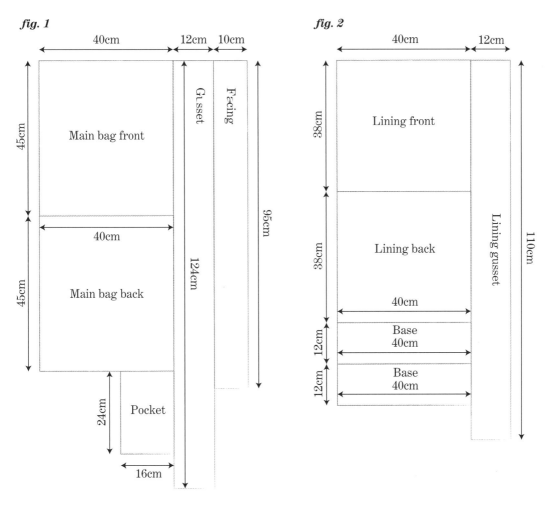

fig. 1

fig. 2

1. Following the measurements given in Fig 1, mark and cut out the main bag pieces from the heavyweight luggage fabric.

2. Following the measurements given in Fig 2, mark and cut out the lining pieces from the canvas fabric.

3. Cut the plastic mesh to measure 9cm × 37cm. Using a stanley knife and a metal ruler, cut the leather strip into six pieces as follows:
Two 55cm × the full width of the leather strip;
Four 5cm × half the width of the leather strip.
Draw the knife over the cut line several times to make the cuts rather than in one single cut.

MAKING THE MAIN BAG

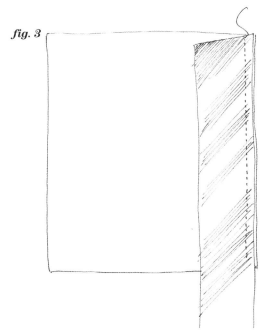

fig. 3

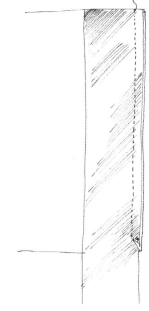

fig. 4

1. With right sides together, pin the gusset to the long side of one of the main bag pieces taking a 1.5cm seam allowance, stopping exactly 1.5cm from the bottom edge of the main bag; reverse stitch to secure the stitching (Fig 3).

2. Lift the presser foot and raise the needle out of the fabric; snip the gusset to the end of the stitching using a sharp pair of scissors (Fig 4).

fig. 5

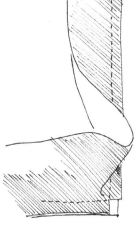

fig. 6

3. Put the needle back into the fabric at the same place, turn the bag 45 degrees and carry on sewing; remember to backstitch to reinforce the corner and make sure you move the gusset fabric out of the way before you start sewing (Fig 5).

4. Repeat for the second corner (Fig 6); if the gusset finishes too long or too short you haven't taken exactly 1.5cm at the corners. Attach the gusset to the other side of the main bag in the same way.

MAKING THE LINING

1. Prepare the main fabric pocket piece and attach to the middle of the lining front placing it 11.5cm from the bottom edge (see Duffel Bag, p149, Figs 9–12 for more instruction on making a pocket). Sew together the gusset lining first to one side of the lining then to the other as described for the main bag, but this time leave a 20cm opening at the bottom edge of one side of the lining (Fig. 7).

fig. 7

The tote bag features a handy inside pocket

CONTINUING WITH THE MAIN BAG

fig. 8

1. Sew the facing piece together along its short edges taking a 1.5cm seam allowance. With right sides together, pin and sew the facing to the top of the main bag, making sure all the seams are open and flat (Fig 8).

fig. 9a

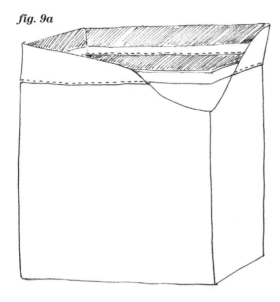

fig. 9b

fig. 9c

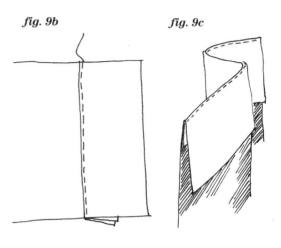

2. Under stitch all the way around the facing (Fig 9a). Press the seams open then press over to the facing side; edge stitch along the facing side (Fig 9b). The under stitching will only show on the inside facing and not on the front of the bag and it will help to keep the facing in place on the inside of the bag once the bag is completed (Fig 9c).

fig. 10

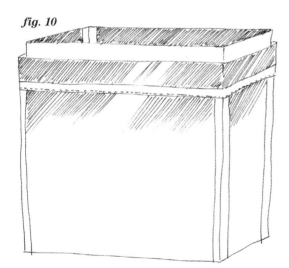

fig. 11a

fig. 11b

fig. 11c

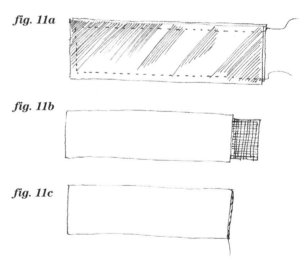

3. Turn the main bag inside out and the lining right side out. Put the lining inside the main bag so that the right sides are together (Fig 10). Pin and sew the tops together making sure that all seams match and remain open and flat.

4. To make the bag bottom, take the lining base pieces and sew together leaving one short edge open (Fig 11a). Trim the corners, turn right side out and slip the plastic mesh inside (Fig 11b). Turn in the 1.5cm seam allowance on the open edge and slip stitch closed (Fig 11c).

MAKING THE BAG HANDLES

fig. 12

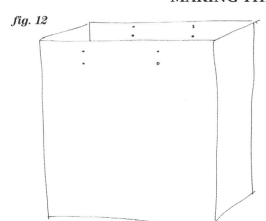

fig. 13

1. Measure and mark the rivet positions onto the main bag: working 9cm from each gusset seam, make a mark 2cm and 5cm from the bag top (Fig 12).

2. Now measure and mark the rivet positions onto the leather handle straps and reinforcing tabs: working on the centre line of each handle strap, make a mark 1cm and 4cm from each end. Mark the reinforcing tabs to match (Fig 13).

3. Using the revolving hole punch, punch out the holes on the leather handles and reinforcing tabs. Using a small pair of sharp scissors (or a tailor's awl if you have one), pierce the holes in the bag. Matching the holes, push the rivets through the handle, the bag and the reinforcing tab, making sure that your handles remain vertical. Hammer closed (Fig 14).

fig. 14

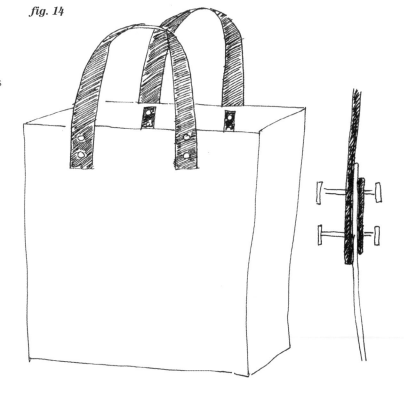

TAILORED SHAWL

A LUXURIOUS AND ELEGANT PURE WOOL WRAP WITH LINING

Our classic woollen shawl with a rolled collar works great over a jacket or thick jumper to be both smart and snug. It even has deep side pockets just where your hands will fall whilst the collar offers a touch of indulgent, cosy luxury. This is a very simple shawl to make. The heart of what you will learn with this project is the importance of thorough pressing. All the great sewing in the world will not lead to a great outcome – only meticulous pressing will.

Materials & Tools You Will Need

- Wool cloth 1.75m × 140cm wide
- Lining fabric 1.75m × 140cm wide
- Medium-weight fusible interfacing 1m
- Matching sew-all thread
- Sewing machine needle size 80
- Tailor's shears
- Small pair of sharp scissors
- Tape measure
- Tailor's chalk

☛ The fabric we have used is a loose weave pure wool and we recommend that you use something similar: with a slightly hairy pile, it is a very forgiving fabric for patch pockets, which can be tricky to make with a very flat fabric.

☛ Use the best lining fabric you can afford – avoid cheap linings which do not hang well. You may need to use a thinner machine needle when sewing the lining pieces together so test stitch first.

☛ To get a perfect result, expect to spend more time pressing than sewing.

☛ Use a clapper (see Pressing Matters, p60) on all the finished edges, especially the facings and pockets; alternatively, use a flat smooth piece of hardwood.

☛ A pattern sheet is available at the back of the book; this will need to be enlarged by 175%. The full-size pattern is available to download at www.merchantandmills.com.

☛ Use a 1.5cm seam allowance unless otherwise stated.

If you are using a check wool for your main fabric, pick out a dominant colour for your lining fabric.

Inside Information

Make sure you align your seams at the sewing line, not the fabric edge.

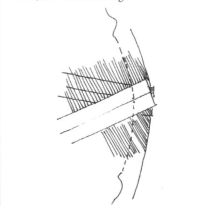

MAKING THE SHAWL

CUTTING AND PREPARING THE FABRIC PIECES

1. Using the pattern sheet provided at the back of the book, cut out the garment pieces as listed below:

2. Snip out the notch marks and mark all the dots on both sides of the fabric pieces.

From the main fabric
Shawl back: cut 1 on the fold
Shawl front: cut 2
Shawl collar facing: cut 2
Neck facing: cut 1 on the fold
Pocket: cut 2

From the lining fabric
Lining back: cut 1 on the fold
Lining front: cut 2
Pocket lining: cut 2

From the fusible interfacing
Collar interfacing: cut 2
Neck interfacing: cut 1 on the fold
Pocket interfacing: cut 2

MAKING AND ATTACHING THE POCKETS TO THE SHAWL FRONTS

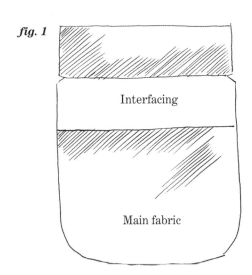

fig. 1

Interfacing

Main fabric

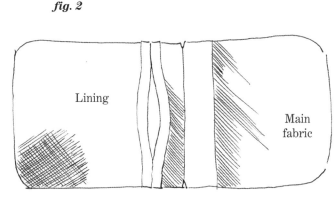

fig. 2

Lining

Main fabric

1. First prepare both pockets. Iron on the interfacing to the wrong side of the pocket below the notch (Fig 1). This will strengthen the top of the pocket.

2. Sew the top of the pocket to the top of the pocket lining leaving a gap for turning through to the right side later (Fig 2).

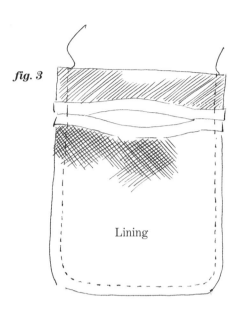

fig. 3

Lining

3. Fold over the pocket at the notches and sew all around the edge (Fig 3).

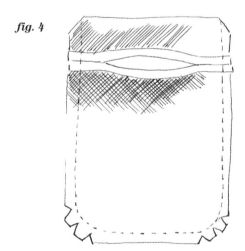

fig. 4

4. Trim the corners and notch the bottom curves (Fig 4). Turn through to the right side and slip stitch the opening closed. Press really well so that the pocket is very neat.

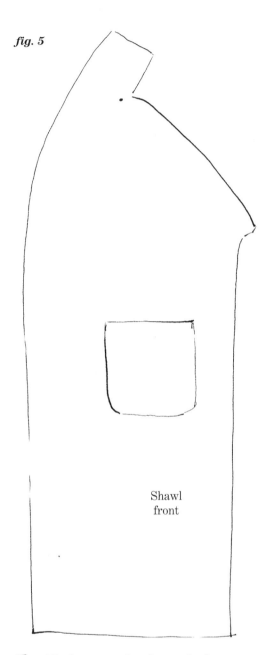

fig. 5

Shawl front

5. Pin the prepared pockets to the fronts as indicated by the pattern markings; edge stitch into place (Fig 5). If you stitch very very close to the edge, you can then press the pocket. If you steam the wool and stretch it a little, the pocket will cover the stitching. Now join the fronts together (in the same way as the interfacings in Fig 6). Press seam open.

JOINING THE FACINGS TO THE MAIN SHAWL

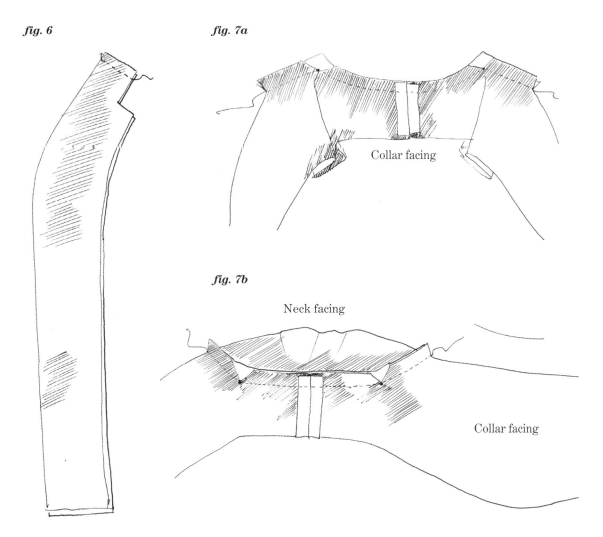

fig. 6

fig. 7a

Collar facing

fig. 7b

Neck facing

Collar facing

1. Iron on the fusible interfacings to the wrong side of the neck and collar facings. Place the collar facings right sides together and sew along the back seam (Fig 6).

2. Sew the neck facing to the collar facing right sides together, referring to Figs 7a and 7b for two different views to help you when turning the corners. Sew along the facing shoulder seam and as you come to the dot reduce the stitch length for extra strength. Stop at the dot, raise the presser foot, lift the needle out of the fabric and, using the small pair of sharp scissors, snip right up to the dot. Put the needle back into the fabric and turn the corner; this will open up the snip to a 'V'. Return to a normal stitch length once you have passed the corner. Repeat at the second corner, and once the stitching is complete, press the seams open really well. Put the completed facing to one side. Once the stitching is complete trim the excess from the corners opposite the snipped 'V's. Press the seams open really well.

fig. 8

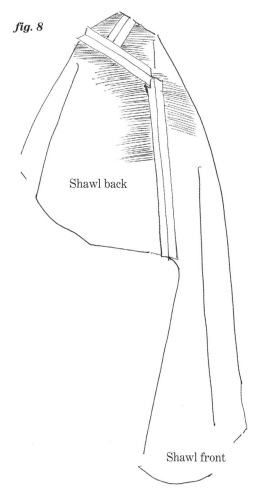

Shawl back

Shawl front

fig. 9

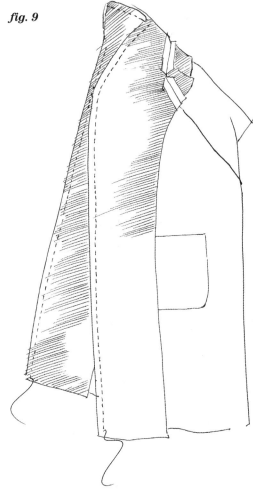

3. With right sides facing, sew the shawl front and shawl back together to make the main shawl (Fig 8) using the same technique for turning the corners as you used when sewing the neck facing to the collar facing in the previous step. Press all the seams open and trim the corners as before.

4. Now sew the completed facing to the main shawl, with right sides together (Fig 9). Press the seam open.

fig. 10

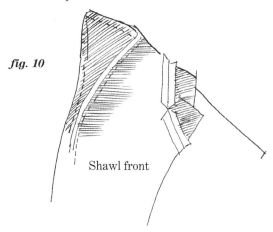

Shawl front

5. Trim the facing side of the seam down to 1cm to reduce bulk (Fig 10).

LINING AND FINISHING THE SHAWL

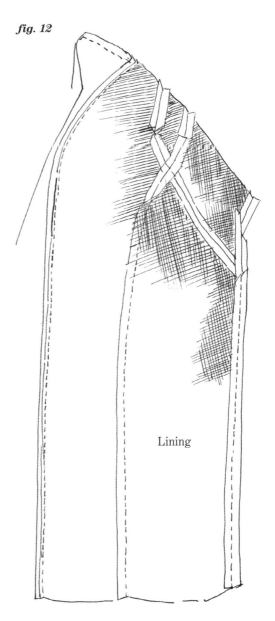

fig. 12

PRESSING TIPS

Steam the finished edge of the sewn fabric and place the clapper on top straightaway (if you don't have a clapper, use a similar lump of hard, flat wood). Press down with all the force you can muster. Leave to cool in place.

fig. 11

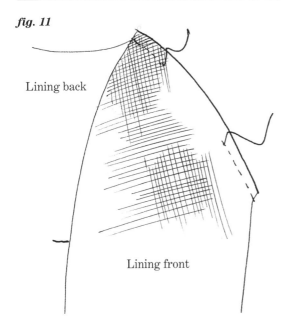

Lining back

Lining front

Lining

1. Sew the lining front and lining back together but leave a gap in one shoulder seam, through which the finished shawl will be turned in step 2 (Fig 11). Press the seams open.

2. With right sides together, sew the lining to facing and main shawl, stitching along the bottom edge too (Fig 12). Press all seams open. Trim corners, turn through to right side and slip stitch lining opening closed. Press well especially around all the edges. Stab stitch through centre back neck seam and top of shoulder seam to hold collar in place.

THE FISHERMAN'S TOP

NAUTICAL BOAT NECK CASUAL TOP

Inspired by the working men of a seabound, fish eating nation, this is an easy to make, lightweight top with a simple boat neck collar and small slits at the sides. It is best made with a crisp cotton for an architectural silhouette or a soft linen for a more relaxed statement. The top is loose fitting like a T-shirt and slips over the head in a jiffy as you splice the mainbrace. We think you are going to like it.

MATERIALS & TOOLS YOU WILL NEED

- Fabric 1.5m × 120cm wide
- Matching sew-all thread
- Standard machine needle size 80
- Hand sewing needle
- Tailor's shears and small pair of sharp scissors
- Tape measure
- Tailor's chalk

☞ For your fabric, choose a medium-weight denim, cotton or linen.

☞ A pattern sheet is available at the back of the book; this will need to be enlarged by 175%. The full-size pattern is available to download at www.merchantandmills.com.

☞ For more on working with patterns review the Patterns chapter, pp40–48.

☞ Use a 1.5cm seam allowance unless stated otherwise.

MAKING THE FISHERMAN'S TOP

CUTTING AND PREPARING THE FABRIC PIECES

1. Using the pattern sheet provided at the back of the book, cut out the following garment pieces:

Top back: cut 2
Top front: cut 1 on the fold
Back collar: cut 1 on the fold
Front collar: cut 1 on the fold

2. Transfer pattern markings to the fabric pieces and snip the notches.

3. Finish all shoulder and side seams on the top back and top front pieces with a zigzag stitch (alternatively, overlock).

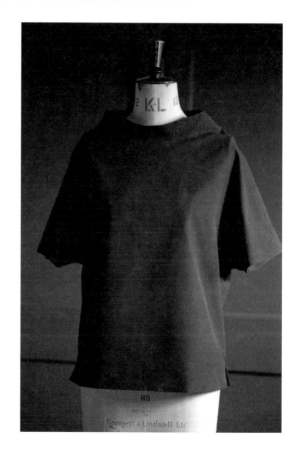

The fisherman's top, shown here in black mid-weight organic cotton.

STITCHING THE COLLAR

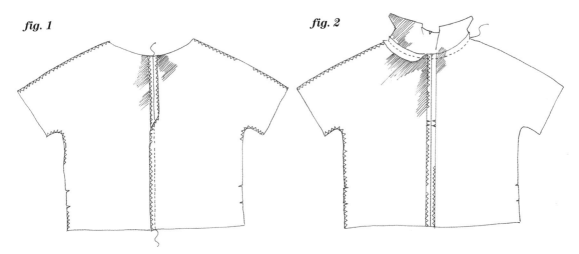

fig. 1

fig. 2

1. Place the top back pieces together with right sides facing; pin and sew up the back seam, then press the seam open (Fig 1).

2. Pin the back collar to the joined back piece, right sides facing, taking care to align the notches. Sew the collar onto the back piece and press the seams open really well (Fig 2). Now join the front collar to the front piece in the same way.

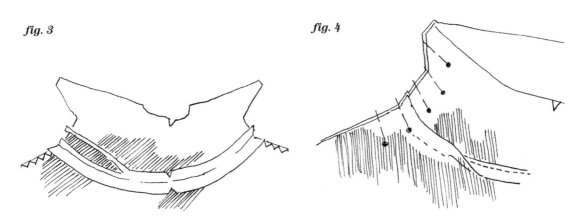

fig. 3

fig. 4

3. Working on both the back and front pieces, trim the inside collar seam down to 5mm (Fig 3), before pressing both seams up onto the collar.

4. Pin the front and back shoulder and collar seams together with right sides facing. Make sure that the collar and neck seams are both facing upwards (Fig 4) and line up the front and back perfectly. Pin right through the seam to ensure that it will be held securely in place as you stitch. The neckline is such an important feature of the finished top that you want to make sure you get this right.

fig. 5

fig. 6a

fig. 6b

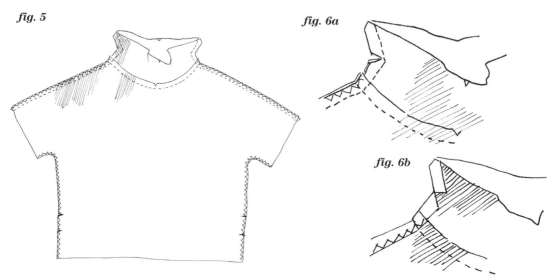

5. Stitch the front and back shoulder and collar seams together, first along one side, then the other, removing pins as you go (Fig 5).

6. Snip a large V into the V section at either side of the collar – this will reduce the bulk when the collar is folded over (Fig 6a). Press all seams open and flat. Press really well (Fig 6b).

fig. 7

7. Fold over the collar and press into position (Fig 7).

JOINING SIDE SEAMS, HEMMING AND FINISHING

fig. 8

fig. 9

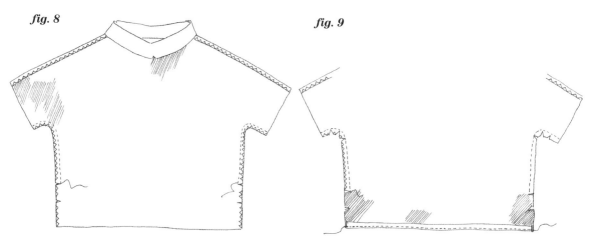

1. Sew the side seams, stopping at the first notch (Fig 8).

2. Turn over the bottom edge by 1cm and topstitch into place (Fig 9). Clip the underarm seam to remove bulk.

fig. 10

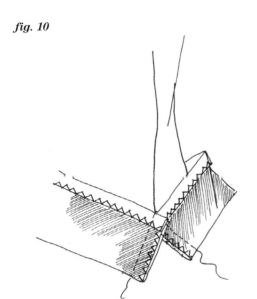

fig. 11a

fig. 11b

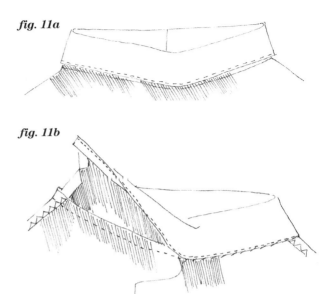

3. Turn the top to the right side. Turn over the hem at the bottom notches. Pin and sew the slits (Fig 10). Trim off the bottom corners. Turn through and carefully poke out the corners. Press nice and flat.

4. Turn the top inside out. Turn under the edge of the collar by the 1.5cm seam allowance and edge stitch to hold the seam allowance in place (Fig 11a). Slip stitch to the neck seam (Fig 11b).

fig. 12

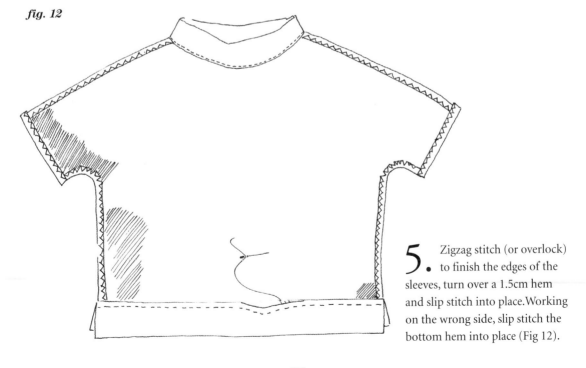

5. Zigzag stitch (or overlock) to finish the edges of the sleeves, turn over a 1.5cm hem and slip stitch into place. Working on the wrong side, slip stitch the bottom hem into place (Fig 12).

INDEX

MERCHANT & MILLS

Merchant & Mills is a creative partnership on a mission to return high end fashion to its rightful owners; you, the sewing public. We have a great respect for craftsmanship and the importance of quality in construction, cloth and tools. The company has a strong emphasis on graphic design to show consistent attentiveness in all we do.

Seasoned dressmaker Carolyn Denham is the driving force to get you all sewing. She cuts the patterns, sources everything and keeps order. Partner Roderick Field makes sure the Merchant & Mills philosophy is properly expressed in words, pictures and brand identity.

Merchant & Mills is stocked by high end stores throughout the world including Liberty, London and the Victoria and Albert museum.
www.merchantandmills.com

Much as we would like to take all the credit for this wonderful book, we have been told to tell the truth instead. The Studio kept running, correspondence was answered and most deliveries went out on time – because we had back up:

THE BOOK TEAM
We would like to thank Amy, Katie, Cheryl and Gemma for all their hard work and patience.

THE TRADES
Tom and Eva at UK Grade, Sally Ward and Sue Thompson, Paul Barrow, Karen Parry.

THE SUPPORTERS
THE SIBLINGS: Stephen, Jacqueline, Ian, Alice, Maggie, Zoe and the might as well be a sister, Sarah.

THE IN-LAWS: Andrew, Bruce, Mark. Naz and Rogers.

Elizabeth Roberts, Dave and Annette, Ewan the Postmaster, Doris and Derek, Rick, Haley, Jaspar, Maud and Otti Field. Barry Morgan.

THE LABOURERS
Sheenagh, Jess, Norma, Sam and Molly.

AND FINALLY
To Mother Denham for all her years of patient teachings that have led to this book and to Dad for being Dad.

The Field parents RIP. We trust they would be proud.

This edition published in the United Kingdom in 2015 by
Pavilion
43 Great Ormond Street
London
WC1N 3HZ

Design and text copyright © Collins & Brown 2012
Photography © Roderick Field 2012

ISBN 978-1-908449-09-2

A CIP catalogue for this book is available from the British Library.

10 9 8 7

Reproduction by Rival Colour Ltd, UK
Printed and bound by 1010 Printing International, Ltd.

www.pavilionbooks.com